RECEIVING FROM HEAVEN

DESTINY IMAGE BOOKS BY KEVIN L. ZADAI

It's Rigged in Your Favor

Supernatural Finances

The Agenda of Angels

Praying from the Heavenly Realms

RECEIVING FROM HEAVEN

INCREASING YOUR CAPACITY TO RECEIVE
FROM YOUR HEAVENLY FATHER

KEVIN L. ZADAI

DESTINY IMAGE® PUBLISHERS, INC.

P.O. Box 310, Shippensburg, PA 17257-0310

"Promoting Inspired Lives."

This book and all other Destiny Image and Destiny Image Fiction books are available at Christian bookstores and distributors worldwide.

Cover design by Eileen Rockwell
Interior design by Terry Clifton

For more information on foreign distributors, call 717-532-3040.

Reach us on the Internet: www.destinyimage.com.

ISBN 13 TP: 978-0-7684-5404-8
ISBN 13 eBook: 978-0-7684-5405-5
ISBN 13 HC: 978-0-7684-5407-9
ISBN 13 LP: 978-0-7684-5406-2

For Worldwide Distribution, Printed in the U.S.A.

1 2 3 4 5 6 7 8 / 24 23 22 21 20

DEDICATION

I dedicate this book to the Lord Jesus Christ. When I died during surgery and met with Jesus on the other side, He insisted that I return to life on the earth and that I help people with their destinies. Because of Jesus' love and concern for people, the Lord has actually chosen to send a person back from death to help everyone who will receive that help so that his or her destiny and purpose is secure in Him. I want You, Lord, to know that when You come to take me to be with You someday, it is my sincere hope that people remember not me, but the revelation of Jesus Christ that You have revealed through me. I want others to know that I am merely being obedient to Your heavenly calling and mission, which is to reveal Your plan for the fulfillment of the divine destiny for each of God's children.

ACKNOWLEDGMENTS

In addition to sharing my story with everyone through the books *Heavenly Visitation: A Guide to the Supernatural, Days of Heaven on Earth: A Guide to the Days Ahead, A Meeting Place with God, Your Hidden Destiny Revealed, Praying from the Heavenly Realms: Supernatural Secrets to a Lifestyle of Answered Prayer, The Agenda of Angels, Supernatural Finances, It's All Rigged in Your Favor,* and *You can Hear God's Voice,* the Lord gave me a commission to produce this book, *Receiving from Heaven.* This book addresses some of the revelations concerning the areas that Jesus reviewed and revealed to me through the Word of God and by the Spirit of God during several visitations. I want to thank everyone who has encouraged me, assisted me, and prayed for me during the writing of this work, especially my spiritual parents, Dr. Jesse Duplantis and Dr. Cathy Duplantis. Special thanks to my wonderful wife Kathi for her love and dedication to the Lord and to me. Thank you, Sid Roth and staff, for your love of our supernatural Messiah, Jesus. Thank you, Warrior

Notes staff, for the wonderful job editing this book. Thank you, Destiny Image and staff, for your support of this project. Special thanks, as well, to all my friends who know about *Receiving from Heaven* and how Jesus would want us to live in this truth in the next move of God's Spirit!

CONTENTS

INTRODUCTION

WHEN JESUS ASKED ME TO WRITE THIS PARTICUlar book, *Receiving from Heaven*, He wanted me to emphasize that the heavenly Father has sent all that we need for life and godliness through Jesus Christ. The Lord notified me that we are excelling in our giving but lacking in our receiving. He further explained that the difficulty with most of His children is placing themselves in a position to receive from their loving, heavenly Father. The secrets that I share in this book are very important for your life in the supernatural realm in these last days. The final move of God's Spirit has begun and we must accept the fact that God is a good, gracious heavenly Father who gives to His children freely. He has already provided for your every need and it is time for us to be *Receiving from Heaven!*

KEVIN L. ZADAI, TH.D.

Chapter 1

SET UP TO RECEIVE

*And when he heard that it was Jesus of
Nazareth, he began to cry out and say, "Jesus,
Son of David, have mercy on me!"*

—MARK 10:47

THE LORD SPOKE TO ME AND SAID, "Kevin, the
problem is not in the shipping process. I have a distribution center. I have everything that anyone is ever going
to need. If I do not have it, I will make it for you. I am the
Almighty God. I have plenty of angels, I have plenty of provision, I am fine, I am ready to send, and I am ready to ship. The
problem is the shipping address; the problem is the receiver."
If you do not receive something, it does not matter if it is at

your door or not, because it is not coming into your house unless you open the door and you bring it in.

Jesus could not do miracles in His hometown because the people there were not receivers. The reason they were not good receivers was because they did not honor the person of Jesus Christ for who He was. To them, He was a carpenter's son, and that is what they got—a carpenter's son. Those who called out, "Jesus, Son of David, have mercy on me" were healed because in calling Him by that title they recognized Jesus as the Messiah. In Nazareth, God brought Jesus to their door, but they did not receive Him. God will bring the answers you need to your door, but you must be set up to receive them.

The Goodness of God

The Gospel is good news. However, if people do not think they are going to hell, then I need to ask them, "What if you are wrong?" There are different stages of talking to people to get them to receive. The bottom line is, for the most part, if you preach the Gospel and you preach the goodness of God, it is going to lead people to repentance.

> *Or do you despise the riches of His goodness, forbearance, and longsuffering, not knowing that the goodness of God leads you to repentance?*
>
> —ROMANS 2:4

Paul said that the goodness of God leads people to repentance. I can preach about hell and scare you into "purchasing" an insurance policy, and you will repent. You will get your fire insurance, but then for the rest of your life, the body of Christ will have to deal with you on that level, which is not a mature level. Do not get me wrong; you will be converted, but the conversion is not understood because, "he who has been forgiven much, loves much" (see Luke 7:47). Mature Christians understand that they have been delivered from many things, not just from the flames of hell, and it has given them a revelation of the goodness of God. Due to the goodness of God being revealed to these Christians, I do not have to deal with them in the same way as the others. They have had a revelation of how good God is, and their love for God has caused them to have a relationship with Him.

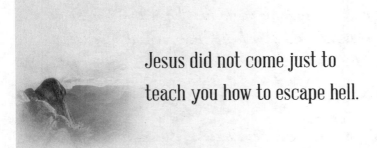

Jesus did not come just to teach you how to escape hell.

Believers who live as if all they did was escape hell are now just waiting for Jesus to return on a white horse. They are waiting for Jesus to take them away from here; this type of believer is living in survival mode. They are buying their food and water in bulk, getting their bomb shelters ready, and waiting for the red dragon to take over (see Rev. 12). That mindset is not born out of relationship with their loving heavenly Father because their actions are based on fear. As a voice to this generation, I have to tell you the truth because we are missing it. Jesus did not come just to teach you how to escape hell, but to show you how to be in relationship with the Father. Jesus came to show you the relationship that *He* has with the Father, and it is summed up here in John 17.

> *That they all may be one, as You, Father, are in Me, and I in You; that they also may be one in Us, that the world may believe that You sent Me. And the glory which You gave Me I have given them, that they may be one just as We are one: I in them, and You in Me; that they may be made perfect in one, and that the world may know that You have sent Me, and have loved them as You have loved Me.*
>
> —JOHN 17:21-23

When you read these verses, Jesus is essentially saying, "Father, the same glory that We share, You are sharing with them that we all may be together as one." We are going to have the revelation of that oneness and share in the glory of God also.

As His divine power has given to us all things that pertain to life and godliness, through the knowledge of Him who called us by glory and virtue, by which have been given to us exceedingly great and precious promises, that through these you may be partakers of the divine nature, having escaped the corruption that is in the world through lust.

—2 PETER 1:3-4

Peter is saying that through God's divine power, exceedingly great and precious promises have been given to us. That is the goodness of God! Through those promises, we can escape the corruption that is in the world through lust and be partakers of the divine nature. That is what we were created to be, as it was in the very beginning in the garden of Eden.

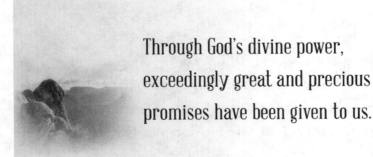

Through God's divine power, exceedingly great and precious promises have been given to us.

THE FOUNDATION OF GOD'S THRONE

I am not being restored so that I can escape from hell. I am being restored so I can walk in the garden with God, my Father. I am not going to hide in my bomb shelter for Him to come and take me home. All the while, the world continues to do what it wants to do, keeping all of the provision and controlling everything down here on earth. I am going to get involved with everything, and I am going to pray in the Spirit in power everywhere I go. I am not afraid to pray, and I will pray that way in front of anyone. I do not care what people think because I am focused on God and the foundation of His throne.

> *Your glorious throne rests on a foundation of righteousness and just verdicts. Grace and truth are the attendants who go before you.*
>
> —PSALM 89:14 TPT

The throne of God is built on the foundations of righteousness, justice, and truth. God's throne is built on His absolute truth. God is not going in there and telling the angels to change this layer, or that He does not like that stone. He is not going to say that justice and holiness are old-fashioned and have to go. God's throne is built on certain characteristics of His kingdom, and He rules and reigns on that throne. When God makes a judgment, there are layers of justice, righteousness, and truth that He is sitting on, and that represents what His decisions are based upon.

Our foundation to receive from Jesus Christ and the Father is based on the fact that we were made *in the image of God*. We need to become great receivers of the grace and the mercy of God. We are never going to be good enough to receive all the goodness that God is going reveal to us. We can never make it any better than what Jesus Christ has already done for us through His blood. The blood of Jesus is not going to be diminished in these last days. There is not a lot of talk about the blood of Jesus anymore because it is offensive. Pastors are told that if they want their church to grow, they should take down the cross in their church and not talk about the blood. Pastors are also told that it's not trendy to talk about hell and that they should remove the altars and have only a certain type of music to not offend people. However, Jesus offended people everywhere He went.

I want to change the way you think and the way you perceive in order to set you up to receive from Heaven. When I was in Heaven, I saw God's way of looking at things and God's way of doing things, and I realized that it matched what was written in the Bible. I realized that we did not need to have a new revelation. We do not need to have a new system; we do not have to have anything like that. We need to focus on the goodness of God and what He has provided for us.

> *You saw who you created me to be before I became me! Before I'd ever seen the light of day, the number of days you planned for me were already recorded in your book.*
>
> —Psalm 139:16 TPT

Why did God send Jesus? It was not only to save you from the flames of hell; that is a big deal, but it is bigger than that. I did not get saved just to escape hell. I got saved because God wrote a book about me before I was born. Psalm 139 also tells you that God has paved the way for your future, and He is standing on it. God also goes behind you to protect you from your past. God's plan for you goes around the whole circumference of your life.

> *You've gone into my future to prepare the way, and in kindness you follow behind me to spare me from the harm of my past. With your hand of love upon my life, you impart a blessing to me.*
>
> —PSALM 139:5 TPT

While in Heaven, I realized that each human being who was ever made was created in the image of God. Spiritually we were made to communicate with God and to walk with God. In Heaven, there is a book written about us that has to do with everyone around us in this life. We are supposed to influence the whole generation that we live in because the plan of God is bigger than just the three feet in front of you and around you. Most people's worlds are three feet in diameter, and it is about me, myself, and I.

In God's eyes, the generations that prayed previously are now getting answers to their prayers through you. They have passed on, but God is answering the prayers of people who have prayed in previous generations, the ones who have labored. You are being used to fulfill those promises, and you may not be conscious of it, but it is still happening. You can do the same thing for the next generation. If you would choose to passionately love God to the point where you obey Him, we can wrap it up in this generation.

> *Jesus replied, "Loving me empowers you to obey my word. And my Father will love you so deeply that we will come to you and make you our dwelling place."*
>
> —John 14:23 TPT

If you would choose to passionately love God to the point where you obey Him, we can wrap it up in this generation.

If we can cooperate with God and allow Him to break the power of demons completely, the worldwide move of God will begin like a flood and continue to flow without end. Jesus was five feet from me when He said, "I do not know when I am coming back because the Father will not tell me. But I can tell you that it is not now because China has to come in, Russia has to come in, and the Middle East has to come in." That harvest will bring the Lord Jesus back. We need to pray for the harvest and for the peace of Israel. Jesus said, "It is up to the church when I come back." The Father wants to send Jesus back for His church, but He also wants the harvest to come in. The Father cannot allow the church to be extracted from this world until this happens.

God's plan is that everyone is to be saved—everyone. No one should go to hell, and yet people are going to hell in droves. God has never sent anyone to hell; He does not do that. The books are written in Heaven as though you are going there. That is your destiny, and it is not predestination like you think; it is simply God's nature. God has called those things that are not as though they were (see Rom. 4:17) because He did not make you for hell. Every person was made in the image of God to go to Heaven and to be redeemed. Just like those who were from Nazareth, there are people today who do not accept Jesus.

We must show people their need for salvation. We need to convince them and let them know that the price has already been paid on the cross, and their role is to come in and accept the plan of God for their life that is written in Heaven. Accept Jesus and His sacrifice and be redeemed by the blood of the Lamb, and then your books are open and you can live them out on earth. However, if you choose not to do this, you are going to hell. That is the Gospel; repent, for the Kingdom of God is at hand.

Chapter 2

HEAVEN'S REWARD SYSTEM

Nevertheless you have done well that you shared in my distress. Now you Philippians know also that in the beginning of the gospel, when I departed from Macedonia, no church shared with me concerning giving and receiving but you only.

—PHILIPPIANS 4:14-15

H ERE IN PHILIPPIANS, PAUL MENTIONS GIVING AND receiving, but we never talk about the receiving part. The Lord told me that most people are generous and they are givers, but our ability to receive needs as much attention. You know you need finances, you need healing, and you need guidance. How do we become good receivers? Jesus showed me that we were created with the desire to be rewarded for our behavior. It is a part of who we are, and our heavenly Father made us this way. The first thing for you to realize is that God has set up a reward system.

> *But without faith it is impossible to please Him,*
> *for he who comes to God must believe that He is,*
> *and that He is a rewarder of those who diligently*
> *seek Him.*
>
> —HEBREWS 11:6

God has set up a reward system in Heaven for people who make the effort to seek Him. God is a rewarder of those who diligently seek Him, and those who seek Him will find Him. Jesus said, "If you get to the place where you love Me passionately, you will obey Me, and when you do that, My Father and I will come and live with you" (see John 14:23). When that happens, you will have the Trinity living inside of you. You will be working with the Trinity because you already have the Holy Spirit inside of you. They are going to start to take notice of everything about you and start to become actively involved in your life. You must yield to God in order for that to happen. Our Father in Heaven wants you to be a good receiver as well as a good giver, and the Spirit of God wants to help you in your weaknesses (see Rom. 8:26). God wants to get you to the place where you can receive from Heaven.

*Not that I seek the gift, but I seek the fruit that
abounds to your account.*
—PHILIPPIANS 4:17

Here in Philippians, the apostle Paul is saying that there
is a reward system. Paul was not just seeking a gift; he was
seeking the fruit that abounded to the believer's account.
Paul wanted them to prosper not only in their finances but
in every area. Did you know that prosperity is not just what
comes into your account? It can also be about what is going
out of your account; you may have a leaky vessel.

Did you know that prosperity is
not just what comes into your
account? It can also be about
what is going out of your account;
you may have a leaky vessel.

I was once living in an especially hot climate, and the
Lord started speaking to me about what I could do to seal up
the air leaks in my house. I did the six things the Lord told
me to do, and I saved hundreds of dollars a month on my elec-
tric bill. I started doing that with everything. I realized that I
could control what goes out of my account, but it helped that
I was receiving information from Heaven. The Lord told me

that it is not just how much is coming in; it is also about what is going out. The Lord asked if I really needed to buy a five-dollar cup of coffee every day. When I said, "no," He told me that they make specialty coffee that you can brew individually instead, and they are only a dollar each. If you allow God to start to speak to you, He is going to start leading you into all truth. Right here in Philippians, Paul is saying, "I want it to abound to you, to be laid up to your account." There is an account and there is a reward system. That is good news!

> *And my God shall supply all your need according*
> *to His riches in glory by Christ Jesus.*
> —PHILIPPIANS 4:19

This verse shows that God has an account. He has a supply, and He is going to take out of that, as Paul said, and give it to you. But it is going to come out of a spiritual account, and it is going to be somehow translated into something material down here on earth. However, it is not always going to come the way you think it is. It might be by saving on what is going out. The point is that spiritual things have to translate into this physical realm. In essence, Paul is saying, "There is an account, and I want you to give, not so that you give to me as an apostle, but I want it to be laid up to your account. God is going to supply all your need according to His riches in glory in Christ Jesus because God has an account for you." There are accounts in Heaven, and God's angels keep track of everything.

My wife and I recently had an experience where we did not want to leave our offices because we had just gotten our studio up and running, and the power of God was so strong there. However, we needed to be at the airport, and so we went because God had sent us. When we travel or when I write a book or teach a class, I expect a big return in *your* life. I want it to be laid up to your account. It is laid up to your account by your discerning who Jesus is. You do not just get a table and chairs because He is not just the carpenters' son. When you need deliverance, you need healing, and you need provision, you call out, "Messiah," or you call out, "Son of David." You do not call out, "Isn't that the carpenters' son?" That was why Jesus' hometown lost out.

When we travel or when I write a book or teach a class, I expect a big return in *your* life. I want it to be laid up to your account.

O Jerusalem, Jerusalem, the one who kills the prophets and stones those who are sent to her! How often I wanted to gather your children together, as

*a hen gathers her chicks under her wings, but you
were not willing!*

—MATTHEW 23:37

Jerusalem also lost out by not recognizing their Messiah. Not long before He was crucified, Jesus spoke to the multitudes. What Jesus was saying here in Matthew 23 was that they did not discern the day of their visitation. You also must discern that He is visiting you, and then you fulfill the receiving end of your covenant with God. Discern right now that God wants to reward you and that He does have a system and that everything you do for Him is rewarded. Even if the person you labored for ignores you, it does not matter because it is out of your hands now. Once you do something for someone, that transaction has happened and spiritually, the reward is laid up in your account. It is so rigged in our favor; Christianity has to get back to this simplicity so that even a child can accept it. Children are encountering Heaven before their parents because they can accept the Kingdom with childlike faith.

WHAT IS IN YOUR HAND?

*Then the Lord asked him, "What is that in your
hand?" "A shepherd's staff," Moses replied.*

—EXODUS 4:2 NLT

The Israelites had fled Egypt, and they were there at the edge of the sea and were trapped. The Egyptian armies were coming, and Moses' people were screaming at him and crying out to God to save them (see Exod. 14:10-22). At that moment, the war got into Moses. The pressure got into him, and then Moses started crying out to God. The Lord was telling Moses to shut up when He asked him, "Why are you crying out to Me?" God told Moses to go down to the water and lift his staff to divide the water supernaturally. It was always meant for Moses to use his staff and for it to be that way, but the war had gotten into Moses. The people transferred the war to Moses and then it neutralized him. That is what happens with you when people start coming to you and they pull you into their emotional realm.

I have friends who are in the hospital right now, and they have death sentences on them. I have already told them they shall live and not die. The Holy Spirit would not let me call them because it has already been spoken. It has already been uttered, and I cannot be pulled into the emotions of losing my friends. I must stay in resurrection power. Even if Jesus shows up late to raise Lazarus from the dead, it does not matter. Jesus showed up at the time He was supposed to, but it was too late for the soulish realm. Jesus always spoiled funerals and bad news. I can call and be a friend and be nice and encourage people in everything, but to me, that is not the staff of Moses in my hand. That is not the donkey jawbone of Samson (see Judg. 15) in my hand that is given by the Word of the Lord.

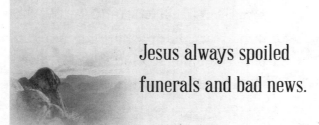

Jesus always spoiled
funerals and bad news.

What happens if God comes to your house and lives with you, and *you* get the Word of the Lord in your own home? That is Christianity. That is not being a prophet; that is simply being a Christian. That is the church of the Lord Jesus Christ, and "the gates of hell will not prevail against it" (see Matt. 16:18). How can you mess that up? I cannot do anything better than what was said there, and I am certainly not going to back off of it. Compromising does not help anyone. You want to have that sharp edge about you so that your life gets in order and then you can help others get their life in order. God is not calling you to compromise, and He is not calling you to reclaim the land that He has already acquired for you.

Some things are futile to sit and talk about. In conversation I can tell people I love them and I am praying for them. But if you want the Word of the Lord from me, you have to let God talk to me. If He does not talk to me, I am not saying anything. Old Testament prophets were stoned when they misinterpreted or spoke from the soul realm. I have the fear of the Lord and I want to speak by the Spirit of God. I want it to be sharp, and I want every devil to know that this guy means business. I want every person in the body of Christ to know that God sets in the church some to be apostles, prophets, evangelists, pastors, and teachers (see Eph. 4:11-13). You do not have to say what you are because they will know you by your fruit (see Matt. 7:16).

REMOVE FEAR THAT YOU MAY RECEIVE

And He saw also a certain poor widow putting in two mites. So He said, "Truly I say to you that this poor widow has put in more than all."

—LUKE 21:2-3

To receive from Heaven, you have to get rid of fear. If God tells you to give or if you want to give of your substance, you cannot be afraid that you are going to be in lack. Jesus shared with me the story of the widow and the two mites. He told me that when He was observing the people coming and giving their offering at the temple, the Pharisees were standing there, as well as the disciples and the poor widow. She came, and she gave her offering and walked away. Everyone else put on a show of their offerings. Jesus pointed her out to the disciples and told them that this woman gave more than anyone because those were her last two mites. Jesus did not go up to her and stop her even though He knew what she had done, but He did brag about her to the disciples. Jesus could have stopped her, and He could have had Judas run after her to give her money, but He did not.

> *So let each one give as he purposes in his heart, not grudgingly or of necessity; for God loves a cheerful giver.*
> —2 CORINTHIANS 9:7

Knowing that Jesus sees everything is the kind of trust you must have with the Lord. When you have determined in your heart what you are going to do, then you will receive your reward. You should not give anything until you have determined in your heart what you want to do, and it seems good to you and the Holy Spirit. That is what the apostle Paul said, "For it seemed good to the Holy Spirit, and to us" (see Acts 15:28). You become a good receiver because you give correctly. Receiving has to do with the fact that you cannot lose. The widow woman could not lose, but she may not have known it. She may have gone home hungry that night and not eaten, but in Heaven everyone knows about her to this day, even on the earth, because she has been written into the Word. She did receive her reward; it was not obvious, but Jesus noted it. God loves a cheerful giver!

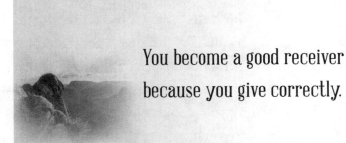

You become a good receiver because you give correctly.

I have gotten to the place where I do not have any need. Recently I looked at one of our personal bank accounts that I have not used since I worked at Southwest Airlines. I thought to myself that there was too much money in there to just be sitting when it could be put to work in some way. The Lord said to me, "I want you to pay a certain person's car off right now." I asked my wife, Kathi, and I could not even finish before she responded, "Yes, let's do it." We paid their car off, and they all started crying. I started to prophesy to them, and I told them that the Lord had called them to ministry, and God was going to use them in a mighty way and wanted to take them out of debt. Their last car had broken down, and the Lord wanted to make it as though it never happened. When God tells you to do something, you should not have a fear of being in need. There is an open Heaven over me because my wife and I obeyed God. You cannot lose because there is a reward system in Heaven, and you are not afraid of being in need.

You cannot do anything out of fear, and you cannot live in fear. You establish in your heart what God is telling you to do, and then you do it, and then you become a good receiver. Angels have been dispatched on your behalf the minute you obey God. You may be trying to figure out if this is too good to be true, and I am telling you it is absolutely true! It is the same principle regarding receiving your healing or receiving your deliverance. In order to get the results, you have to engage with what has been set up. To be a good giver, you have to be a good receiver, so you have to expect that God is going to reward you because He rewards those who diligently seek Him.

RELATIONSHIP DRIVEN FAITH

Ask, and it will be given to you; seek, and you will find; knock, and it will be opened to you. For everyone who asks receives, and he who seeks finds, and to him who knocks it will be opened.

—MATTHEW 7:7-8

In regard to healing, Jesus told me, "When I took the stripes upon My back when I was crucified, I went to the belly of the earth (see Eph. 4:8-10). I bought everything back from satan, *everything*, and I am not going back and going through all of that again. I made sure that I bought everything for everyone. On earth, I went around doing good and healing everyone who was oppressed of the devil." Everyone who came to Jesus got healed. If you seek, you are going to find; if you ask, you are going to receive; and if you knock, the door will be opened. You are not going to hear, "Well, what do you want?" No, the door is going to swing right open. Jesus says that and there is no other discussion, and He did not even mention believing. Believing is essentially a step above what we call faith because of the way we have made faith a system. That system says that if we say it enough, we can convince God by wearing Him out. Our asking God for something is not about a system; it is about a relationship.

> Our asking God for something is not about a system; it is about a relationship.

Relationship goes above what we call faith, and your relationship with God needs to go another step. Relationally, you do not make demands on God—that is not a relationship. There is a part of God that when He tells you something, He does not want you to doubt; He does not want you to question it. However, there are the times when you come to Him and say, "Lord, does this seem good to You? Because a lot has happened. I have been through a lot of warfare. Are we still good with what we have discussed; is this still what You want me to do?" Sometimes people flip out on you and it delays your destiny, and this is what being in relationship with your heavenly Father is about—sharing your life with Him.

> *Therefore we wanted to come to you—even I, Paul, time and again—but Satan hindered us.*
> —1 THESSALONIANS 2:18

Imagine the apostle Paul being hindered by satan, yet here is the account in the Bible. There are dynamics involved in faith, and it is more about your relationship with God. There is a difference. You have to understand that God is not just a system and you are not just working the Word, but *He is working you.* God is a person, and He is right there in your room, and you should not talk *about* Him but rather talk *to* Him. You need to let Jesus live through you. Your giving and receiving from Heaven have to do with your relationship with Him. It is not just about faith as we know it to be.

In the Old Testament, the Hebrew word for *faith* is "relationship," and it had to do with trust. It was about knowing a person so well that you could trust that if they said they were going to do something, you knew that they were going to do it. That is what faith in God is in the purest sense. Faith is knowing God does not lie and knowing that He does not tell you that He will do something and then not do it. If it does not happen, it is because of warfare, but it is not an issue with the sender; the issue is on the receiving end. When your supply is being held up, it has to do with the receiving end. That has to do with you, your warfare, the environment that you live in, and people messing up because people can mess up your destiny. The angels are going to agree with God. Then if *you* agree with God, the angels are ready to go, and God sends them out.

> *When Joshua was near the town of Jericho, he looked up and saw a man standing in front of him with sword in hand. Joshua went up to him and demanded, "Are you friend or foe?" "Neither one," he replied. "I am the commander of the Lord's army." At this, Joshua fell with his face to the ground in reverence. "I am at your command," Joshua said. "What do you want your servant to do?"*
>
> —JOSHUA 5:13-14 NLT

The angels are going to agree with God. Then if *you* agree with God, the angels are ready to go, and God sends them out.

That is why in this verse, when Joshua encountered the warrior angel on the road, he asked the angel, "Are you for us or against us?" The angel replied, "Neither" because the Lord had sent him, and he was on assignment. The angel was not choosing sides because he was on the side of the Lord. As long as Joshua was on the side of the Lord, he was fine. You need to look at all the Scriptures that refer to angels and realize that angels are being sent, and when you are being sent, then you can trust in that.

I was sent back, and I cannot fail because Jesus was five feet from me when He told me that. If that is the way it is, then when you lay hands on the sick, you are not the healer. You are simply laying your hands on people, and you do what you are supposed to do. You get the treadmill out of the box, you turn it on, and you get on it, and God will do the rest, but you have to do what you have to do. You lay hands on the sick. You engage God and His Kingdom, you come against what satan is doing, and every time you encounter satan you hit him over the head with a two-by-four! You nail that demon, and you never give him any rest. You can have him so exhausted that he cannot even talk to you. If you knew how much I know about what I am talking about, you would take these words to heart. These demons cannot function with a Christian who knows what is going on. They cannot function because they have no plan B. When you operate in the Spirit, they do not know how to handle you.

Receiving from Heaven has to do with being in a position where you can hear from God and implement His kingdom down here on the earth. As you know, the world will be turned over to Jesus Christ. The kingdoms of the world will become the kingdoms of our Lord and of His Christ (see Rev. 11:15). Down here, the kingdom is within us and advancing through us, and it is going to happen through the church, through the believers. I am not waiting for one brave soul to do it; I am going to do it. It is time to feel the power of the coming age and let it take you to another level. It is time to manifest God's glory.

Jesus will not stop you from doing what He tells you to do; *only you* are going to stop yourself.

When that poor widow with the two mites put all that she had into the offering, Jesus did not stop her. Jesus will not stop you from doing what He tells you to do; *only you* are going to stop yourself. The Lord has never told me to pray in tongues for a certain number of hours a day, but I knew that my entrance into the supernatural had to do with prayer and with yielding. I knew that putting my flesh under subjection would unlock the entrance. So, I learned how to put my flesh under, even though I love to eat, and I love to go and do things. I have to shut myself in a room and fast and pray in the Spirit, and it is not because God told me to. Sometimes I pray for 14 hours a day because I want to get something from the other realm and bring it to earth knowing that is my part.

The apostle Paul prayed in tongues more than all (see 1 Cor. 14:18). The point is that there are certain things that you are supposed to do. If you do those things, you are going to get results, but you are not being told to do them. When you go to eat, God might want you to miss that meal and go pray, but He is not going to tell you not to eat. You can go and eat because it is your choice, and God is not going to stop you. That is the way God allows it to be in this realm.

When you go to pray, you have to determine in your heart what you want to do and then do it because everything around you will fight you. God is not going to tell you that you need to pray for two hours today; He does not normally do that. However, I noticed that the devil does not want me to pray that long, and I noticed that he does not want me to give either. God does not always tell you that if you do *this*, then *that* is going to happen. You have to determine that yourself, but I have noticed that demons start screaming when I pray in tongues. I notice that when I give to children and people who cannot pay me back that I get so much back that I do not know what to do with it. I notice that when I tithe, I cannot find enough room for what comes in. The floodgates of Heaven are open, and the devourer is rebuked for my sake (see Mal. 3:11). Within the parameters of what God has already said, you have to go further, and He is not going to stop you, but you have to be hooked up to the point where you are a good receiver.

I never pray thinking that I am not going to get an answer. I never pray thinking it is not going to work. You have to purpose in your heart that this is what you are supposed to do and then do it and stick with it, and you will receive it. You have to stay in there with God's intention. That poor widow was not stopped from giving her last. She did it, and she was noted by God, and it can be the same way with you.

Think about where you are in the Lord and where you feel you need to go. Ask yourself this, "Why do I feel like I need that? Why do I feel like I need to go here? Is that the Spirit, or is that my flesh?" Once you determine the parameters that God has put inside of you, and once you have established God's path, know that any opposition you get for that is going to be demonic. This is the key to seeing it through to the point where you receive from Heaven. Once you have determined this is the way it is going to be, then you stay with it. I would prefer that you know before you do anything.

Once I have established that it is God's will to heal me— just like it was when I got my new kidneys, my new liver, and my eyesight returned to normal—the same thing will go for every other part of my body that still needs to be healed. Once I have established *that* is the way it is, then I begin to receive from Heaven. In 1983, I went to the optometrist, and I accepted the fact that I needed glasses and contacts. I remember being driven home, and I was in tears because I did not want to believe that way. I wore those contacts and those glasses until last year. I was in my chair in my study, and the breath of God came on me, and I did not need my contacts anymore. I received my healing in 1983, but there is a war going on down here and a process that I went through. However, in the end, it does not matter what the devil does or says.

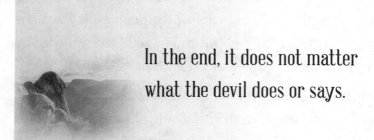

In the end, it does not matter what the devil does or says.

EVERYTHING YOU NEED FOR LIFE AND GODLINESS

Man, even in his best efforts, can be flawed. You cannot make theology out of your encounters or any kind of experience you have. You cannot make a belief system based on what happens to you because we are living in a broken world. We are redeemed in Christ, but we are working out our salvation with fear and trembling (see Phil. 2:12-13). Do not use anything that happens to you to enforce what you believe. What you believe is enforced by the manifestation of God. Jesus told Nicodemus that he could not see the wind, but he could see the results of the wind when it blows through the trees (see John 3:7-8). The result of the wind blowing is that it makes the trees move, and it is the same with the Spirit. You do not see the Spirit of God, but you see the results.

No one can reverse engineer being born again. You cannot be put into a lab and explain being born again and have it analyzed. They cannot tell you how you are different, but you were once lost, and now you are found. Now you are going to Heaven when yesterday you were going to hell. Scientists cannot put you into an environment where they can watch you change, they cannot manufacture the born-again experience, and they cannot reproduce it, and yet it is true.

The very educated apostle Paul said that he determined not to know anything but Jesus Christ and Him crucified (see 1 Cor. 2:2). That was all Paul wanted to know. Paul also said that he did not come to them with enticing words of man's wisdom, but he came in power and demonstration of the Holy Spirit (see 1 Cor. 2:4). The Spirit of Truth promotes truth. Your observations are not good enough. Science's observations are not good enough.

You may feel fine, but the Lord is saying that you need to eat healing Scriptures every day. If that is what God is telling me, and I am fine, then I am stocking up because I do not want to have to rattle through my healing Scriptures on the way to the emergency room in the ambulance, wondering what happened to me. It does not have to be that way. If the Lord is telling you now to take in those healing Scriptures, then do it every morning because it is preventive medicine!

Everything we could ever need for life and com-
plete devotion to God has already been deposited
in us by his divine power. For all this was lavished
upon us through the rich experience of knowing
him who has called us by name and invited us to

come to him through a glorious manifestation of his goodness.

—2 PETER 1:3 TPT

Peter is saying here that everything you need for life and godliness is inside of you. What then is holding you back? God is sending, but you are not receiving, but now it just got better because it is inside of you already. We have everything we need deposited inside of us, and we are seeking outwardly for manifestation. Scripture says that all creation is waiting for the manifest sons of God to be revealed (see Rom. 8:19). God came through Jesus Christ, who died for you and then deposited everything you need for life and godliness inside of you. The anointing of the Holy Spirit lights that on fire because you have been given everything you need.

I have given up everything to do what the Lord has asked me to do, and it should be this way with you also. If you are in Christ, then you should have the fullness of the manifestation of it without *seeking* the manifestation; it should just happen. You can ask my employees; they see miracles every single day with the ministry. These miracles are signs and wonders to an unbelieving generation. There is something that wants to manifest through you, but it is a Person—it is the truth. The truth is that there are no limitations in the Spirit of God. The limitations are based on this realm. It is more about you yielding than building. It is more about being a sailboat and letting God blow through your sails and sending you where He wants you to go. It is not about getting your high-octane outboard motorboat going and being driven. I am not driven, I am led, and I am a lamb and not a goat or a cow.

> *For as many as are led by the Spirit of God, these*
> *are sons of God.*
> —ROMANS 8:14

The Spirit leads me, and that makes me a son of God, according to this Scripture. Those who are led by the Spirit of God are sons of God, but those who yield to the flesh cannot please God (see Rom. 8:8). The flesh is an enemy of the Spirit. The reason why you are being robbed and why you are not receiving is because the flesh has disqualified you. It is keeping you out of the realm of the Spirit because in the flesh, in your carnal nature, you cannot please God.

Everyone says that their carnal nature is gone. Well, then why did you kick your car when it did not start, and why did you throw a tantrum? You have to yield to the Spirit, and this should be basic Christianity, but it is not. Everything you have for life and godliness has already been provided for you.

YOU *CANNOT* FAIL!

When Jesus sent me back to my body, I did not want to go. Jesus looked at me and said, "If you go and do this, you will not fail; you cannot fail." I wanted Him to say that again because it was hard to comprehend. I quoted Mark 9:23: "If you believe, nothing shall be impossible to you." And Jesus said, "There is no one up here limiting you. Everyone in Heaven loves you and believes in you. No one has ever doubted you. Who told you that you could not do what you know you are supposed to do? It has not been God because God is not limiting you." Jesus made sure I understood that if I went back, I could not fail.

No one has ever told me the idea that I could not fail. I realized that the flesh is what limits us; how we filter things and how we grasp things is how we live. We need to grasp the truth. When I was with Jesus, I was looking at His beard because it was perfect. His hair was three feet long, and Jesus was exceptional beyond words. As I was looking at Him, Jesus was talking to me about how I was formed in my mother's womb and how they wrote a book about me before I was born. Everything about me was written down in Heaven already.

I was looking into Jesus' eyes, and He let me walk right into them; I went inside of Him. I saw how Jesus thought of me and how I was formed in my mother's womb, so I was not an accident. When I came back out, I was looking at Jesus' face, and I was looking at His beard, and I thought, "Who would ever pluck that beard out? Who would ever slap this man? Who would ever crucify Him?" Jesus is so kind, He is so irresistible, and yet if He spoke about another universe, it would form. I cannot imagine someone meeting Jesus and not accepting Him, even the vilest sinner, because He is so irresistible.

You've gone into my future to prepare the way, and in kindness you follow behind me to spare me from the harm of my past. With your hand of love upon my life, you impart a blessing to me. This is just too wonderful, deep, and incomprehensible! Your understanding of me brings me wonder and strength.

—Psalm 139:5-6 TPT

I cannot imagine someone meeting Jesus and not accepting Him, even the vilest sinner, because He is so irresistible.

Jesus works this wonderful salvation for us and writes a book about us in Heaven before we are ever born. Jesus told me that if I go back I cannot fail and that He is going ahead of me, according to Psalm 139. Jesus has already paved the way for me, and He will stand with me. At the time of writing this book, it has been 26 years since Jesus came into the operating room with me. For 23 years, I was not released to talk about it. In the 23rd year after my heavenly encounter, I wrote a book about my experience and retired from the airlines where I worked, and I have not stopped since.

I am here to tell you what you need to do because the move of God has started, and it is a huge, powerful move that will not stop. It is a culmination of all the moves of God, but it does not involve heroes. Jesus told me that the year 2020 is the year of perfect vision. Jesus told me that the church is getting its strength back and getting His vision back. The people of God are going to have discernment like they never have before. You are going to look at some and say, "That is not right." You will be praying in tongues and say, "Do not touch me. I do not need you to lay hands on me; you need to lay hands on yourself." You will not tolerate anything anymore.

You will no longer want to seek an encounter; you will want to seek *transformation*. You want to be a transformed son or daughter of the living God. The angels that are helping you right now will work for you for the rest of your life. They will be assigned to you and do whatever you tell them to do in the next millennium reign with Christ (see Rev. 20:4-6). There is nothing to wait for anymore. Go ahead and qualify for what you are called to do and do it down here on earth. The angels assigned to you are here to wrap it up. I am through with practicing and waiting for the next encounter so that I can make it through another day. I am not living from encounter to encounter anymore. Wherever I go, and wherever you go, we are the next encounter. I do not want you just to make it, because that is not God's plan for you.

I was 31 years old, and I died on the operating table. Jesus was right there and took me and showed me how things operate in Heaven. After I was there for a little while, I thought that I wanted to meet Elijah, I wanted to go to the city, and I wanted to go to the throne room. However, Jesus was telling me how to live down here on earth and how to beat the daylights out of the devil every single day. He told me how to beat him at his own game and win against him. After the sixth or seventh subject that Jesus went through with me without even giving me a break to talk, I started to realize that He was prepping me to go back. Jesus was not talking about anything that I wanted to talk about, like where the ark of the covenant is or UFOs or dinosaurs.

What Jesus is speaking to you is so rigged in your favor. When I came back into my flesh, I remembered that Jesus told me that He was going be with me and that I was to repeat what He was saying to me. I had all of these scholarly degrees hanging on my wall, and afterward I took them down because I realized I did not know anything. Three years ago, when I started to talk about my experience, the world opened up to me, and miracles began happening and continuing to happen, and we are just getting started.

You must receive what is in you; it does not get any better than that because it is so rigged in your favor. God says, "Okay, here is what I want you to do, and this is who you are." It is already written in Heaven, and you have everything you need for life and godliness, and you sit there, and you ask what your next step is. The next step is that you have to take hold of those things which Christ has taken hold of for you. If that sounds familiar, it is because that is what Paul said to the Philippians.

Not that I have already attained, or am already perfected; but I press on, that I may lay hold of that for which Christ Jesus has also laid hold of me.

—Philippians 3:12

I read how Paul reached up and grabbed hold of Christ. It is like he has a hold of Jesus' ankles, and I take hold of Paul. I am taking hold of that which Paul has taken hold of for me. Jesus has taken hold of the Father, and I take hold of Him, and I have the Father. Every truth that is written, the Holy Spirit wants to take it and make it part of you, and it becomes manifestation. However, the manifestation is not an experience; it is a change. It means that you are not the way you were before because you have totally changed. It then becomes easy for you to do the right thing. If you are not there yet, I understand that, but you will learn.

There are certain things you do not do, but the limitations are based on your physical body and your mind and the limitations that are on this realm down here where you live. However, in the Spirit, the Holy Spirit has never limited you. Do you know the Holy Spirit has never had one thought of defeat? He does not even know it. The Holy Spirit has been placed inside of you, so every time you see someone in need, you want to meet that need, and you want to pray for them and see them healed. You are blown away when they are not healed, and you are blown away when you pray for provision and it does not come. The reason is that inside, you are made in the image of God, you are born again, and you are a new creature, a new species in Christ. *"Old things have passed away; behold, all things have become new"* (2 Cor. 5:17). Everything that you need for life and godliness is deposited in you. The limitations are based on this realm. Paul said, "I long to come to you, but satan hindered me."

> *Therefore we wanted to come to you—even I, Paul, time and again—but Satan hindered us.*
>
> —1 THESSALONIANS 2:18

Jesus said, "A prophet is without honor in his own hometown" (see Matt. 13:57). Jesus could not even heal a sniffle in His hometown because they did not discern who He was. The Son of God was limited by unbelief. I have come back to destroy unbelief and make Jesus something that everyone can understand and live. Everyone needs Jesus. When I looked at Jesus, no one would reject Him, and I cannot believe that anyone hates Him. Jesus thought of you, and He breathed you into your mother's womb, and He wrote a book about you, and everything that you need is inside of you.

> *As a result of this, he has given you magnificent promises that are beyond all price, so that through the power of these tremendous promises you can experience partnership with the divine nature, by which you have escaped the corrupt desires that are of the world.*
>
> —2 PETER 1:4 TPT

You need to meditate on this Scripture all the time because this is your world. The angels that I met have never once thought they were going to fail when they have been sent to help. The angels are here to assist those who are going to inherit salvation (see Heb. 1:14). The angels around you do not think they are going to fail. The Holy Spirit inside of you has never once thought of failure. The Father, who wrote your book in Heaven, has never thought you are going to fail. Everything is working in your favor. You have to judge by the truth and not the facts.

The angels around you do not think they are going to fail. The Holy Spirit inside of you has never once thought of failure.

I am not saying you are not going to have trouble. I thoroughly enjoy it when the devil pops his head up. When I was in my second year of college, I was a security officer for the college that I was attending, and I had to work from midnight to 7 AM. I worked alone, and I had to be armed. If anybody came on the property during the night, they had to come through me to get on the campus, or they were trespassing. Trespassers would either be turned in or arrested.

This one night, I got a call and went out there. There was a guy totally full of demons and drunk, so I grabbed him and took him to my office and called the city police to come and get him. I was sitting there staring at him, praying in tongues waiting for the police to come. He said, "Don't do that." I answered, "Do what?" "That," he said, referring to my speaking in tongues. What was happening was the spiritual temperature was starting to increase, not because I was looking for an encounter but because I *am* an encounter, and you are too. The Kingdom of God was advancing and raising the spiritual temperature of the room. Within moments of praying, at least 15 different demonic voices began speaking through that guy without his lips moving. I called my friend, and I said, "Get down here. I got a hot one!" When he got there, I told him to preach on the blood of Jesus. My friend pulled out his Bible and started preaching to this guy about the blood of Jesus and those demons started screaming and began leaving him. I knew who to call because my friend could start preaching at the drop of a hat, and today he is a pastor.

The temperature begins to get increasingly higher in the spirit realm because the Spirit of God is allowed to invade you, invade your space, and then invade others. There is an encounter that happens, but it is not something you are seeking; it is something you are. As the apostle Peter said, we are partakers of the divine nature (see 2 Pet. 1:4). How much more powerful can you get than that? Why do the demons start to manifest? It is because the realm that you have become part of is in direct opposition to the realm that they are in, and things start to happen. You know that you carry the blessing, and you have to receive this by faith, but your faith is based on your relationship with God. We must yield to what is on the inside, which is Christ in you the hope of glory (see Col. 1:27).

Since these virtues are already planted deep within, and you possess them in abundant supply, they will keep you from being inactive or fruitless in your pursuit of knowing Jesus Christ more intimately. But if anyone lacks these things, he is blind, constantly closing his eyes to the mysteries of our faith, and forgetting his innocence—for his past sins have been washed away. For this reason, beloved ones, be eager to confirm and validate that God has invited you to salvation and claimed you as his own. If you do these things, you will never stumble. As a result, the kingdom's gates will open wide to you as God choreographs your triumphant entrance into the eternal kingdom of our Lord and Savior, Jesus the Messiah.

—2 PETER 1:8-11 TPT

Peter is saying that if anyone lacks these things, he is blind. Can you imagine a pastor saying that to you today? This age of extreme grace makes people think that they can do anything they want. You cannot. Peter is saying, "No, if you are inactive, you are blind. Show me and validate your faith in what you do."

Or what man is there among you who, if his son asks for bread, will give him a stone? Or if he asks for a fish, will he give him a serpent?

—MATTHEW 7:9-10

Jesus, in this verse, is comparing your earthly father to your heavenly Father. Your earthly father would not give you a snake if you asked for bread. Well, God the Father is not going to do that either; that is what Jesus is saying. I am tired of religious people telling us what God is and what He is not, and they are not even going by the Word of God. Jesus came to reveal the Father (see Matt. 11:27). Jesus only said what His Father said, and He only did what His Father did. Jesus sent the Holy Spirit, and He said when the Spirit of Truth comes, He is not going to speak on His own (see John 16:13). The Holy Spirit is only going to speak what the Father tells Him to speak. The Spirit of God is going to speak to you what the Father is saying, and that is called ministry.

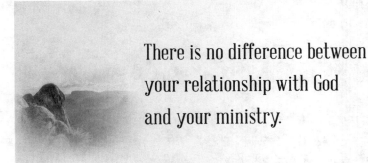

There is no difference between your relationship with God and your ministry.

There is no difference between your relationship with God and your ministry, and it is not a profession. Jesus' ministry was doing the will of the Father, and in that was the manifestation. Jesus was not seeking manifestation; it was who He was and who His Father was.

GOD YOUR PROVIDER

Now to Him who is able to do exceedingly abun-dantly above all that we ask or think, according to the power that works in us, to Him be glory in the church by Christ Jesus to all generations, forever and ever. Amen.
—EPHESIANS 3:20-21

Whatever you can ask or think, God is able to do above that. To be a good receiver, you have to know that God is your provider. He can do exceedingly, abundantly above what we can ask or think, but how does He do it? God does it according to His power that works in us. We do not even have to go somewhere because it is already in us. You need to get ahold of this and turn the tables on the devil.

GIVE IT TO GOD

We are to present our bodies as a living sacrifice—not a dead one, but a living sacrifice—holy and acceptable unto Him, which is our reasonable service (see Rom. 12:1). There is an aroma that comes off of you when you sacrifice or when you walk away from sin. When you walk away, and you choose not to defend yourself. When you could say a hundred things, and you say nothing. There is an aroma that is released.

When people do you wrong and you forgive them, you are releasing them from the situation. Some people are going to wish that they had dealt with you because then they would not have had to deal with God. Forgiveness is better for you because when you forgive, you are released, and then you release that person to God, who then takes up the case. When you release them, the case goes to the higher court, and you do not even have to show up anymore because it is no longer yours. Jesus gave Himself up as an offering, and He said, *"Father, forgive them, for they do not know what they do"* (Luke 23:34). Jesus released it to God the Father, and then He died, but He was coming back. When you start to get to the point where you find yourself in impossible situations and it looks like it is over and you have failed, you can say, "I will be back," because you will be.

Chapter 3

Walking in Your Authority

But as many as received Him, to them He gave the right to become children of God, to those who believe in His name: who were born, not of blood, nor of the will of the flesh, nor of the will of man, but of God.

—John 1:12-13

IN THIS VERSE, THE WORD FOR *RIGHT* MEANS "POWER." He gave them the *power* to become children of God. There are two different Greek words used for power—one is *dunamis* and one is *exousia,* and they are both translated as "power." *Dunamis* has to do with a display of power or brute power. *Exousia* has to do with authority. Someone in authority does not have to use brute strength because the authority that is behind him is enough for you to say, "Yes, sir, I'll do whatever you say." You know that there will be consequences to disobeying. The word *exousia* is used here in John. "To them that believed He gave the *authority* to become children of God." Every devil in hell knows your authority, but they also know whether *you* know it or not.

Jesus was the Son of God, and He did not have to defend Himself, and the devils knew it. Jesus breathed on the disciples and said, *"Receive the Holy Spirit"* (John 20:22). He said to them, "I give you authority over demons and over the sick" (see Mark 16:17-18). Then Jesus sent out the 70, and those people came back and were surprised that they actually had results. They said, "The demons listen to us" (see Luke 10:17). There were dynamics at play there because they were not in full faith, but miracles still happened because it had to do with the authority that was imparted to them. God can manifest Himself through His Word just by you speaking it.

The centurion was complimented as having the greatest faith of all because he said, "Lord, You do not need to come to my house, just speak the Word. I am a man under authority, in authority, and I understand authority" (see Matt. 8:8-10). The authority to become the sons of God is of great significance. It is so much more than what you can do by brute force or even the gifts of the Spirit, which do not even belong to you. You will have to turn in the gifts of the Spirit at the end of your life. You do not get any credit for operating in them because it is not you; it is the Holy Spirit in you.

You should not seek after manifestation. *You* should be manifesting. The Holy Spirit should have free rein and will over you, in you, and through you, and with that comes authority. When he looks into your eyes, the devil knows if you know your authority in Christ. He will have second thoughts when you stare him in the eye and say, "You think you can take me? Come on." That is what I do, and that devil will not come because he sees Jesus there and sees me lit up like a flame. Those demons will know if *you know* who you are in Christ Jesus.

> *But each one is tempted when he is drawn away by his own desires and enticed. Then, when desire has conceived, it gives birth to sin; and sin, when it is full-grown, brings forth death.*
> —JAMES 1:14-15

The devil has to try to draw you out into his arena because it is his only chance of overcoming you. He tries to seduce you and pull you away because satan cannot win on your ground. James says, "You are pulled away by your own desires."

All creation is groaning for the sons of God to be revealed. They are groaning because they fell with us, and it was not their choice. This fallen world is broken, but we can operate in it if we learn how to operate in the Spirit first. Then we have to go to work and be a manifestation of God and His love.

God gave us the authority to be sons of God on earth, and we need to receive it and walk in it.

SET APART BY HOLY FIRE

Come out from among them and be separate, says the Lord. Do not touch what is unclean, and I will receive you.

—2 CORINTHIANS 6:17

I wanted to settle the questions that I had about holiness. I had thought that holiness was behavior. I did not understand how I can be holy and set apart, but I cannot affect other people in holiness, yet they can affect me. I fasted, and I prayed, and I asked the Lord to settle this. What I found is that holiness is when God makes you come out from among everyone else because you are His special possession. A possession that God purchased, setting you apart for His purpose. You are His private stock. God did the same with Israel when He put His name on them (see 2 Chron. 6:6). When Israel messed up, God sent an angel and told them not to provoke the angel because the angel would not tolerate their sin either. We are reminded in the New Testament not to be like the Israelites who, through their unbelief, fell in the desert dead (see Heb. 3:16-19).

For you are a holy people to the Lord your God; the Lord your God has chosen you to be a people

for Himself, a special treasure above all the peoples
on the face of the earth.

—DEUTERONOMY 7:6

I saw that God has set us apart as His personal private showing and that He wants us for His own. Holiness and holy fire have to do with the separation that happens. We are a holy nation under God, and we display His glory and the people of the earth see us (see Isa. 55:5). Scripture says that "The nations are among you because I am your God because you have chosen to obey Me and live and be blessed by Me" (see Exod. 19:5). Many nations will come to you and borrow, but you will not borrow from any of them (see Deut. 28:12). "This is to establish My covenant that people will know on the earth that I am your God." The covenant was established so that God could show Himself through His people.

In the New Testament, we have a better covenant with better promises; God has bought us and now owns us. When we become born again, there begins a struggle in the spirit. This struggle in the spirit is to stop you from being exclusively God's where you have authority. Satan is warring with you, and he is trying to get you into his ring where he can win against you. If you tell him, "No, you come to me," he will not come. Satan does not know what to do with a Christian who knows who they are because he has no plan B. The authority you walk in is based on ownership, and it is based on covenant.

Not long ago, my wife and I both woke up in the middle of the night and then heard a scream in our house. We were the only ones home, so I went through the house from room to room and found nothing. I asked the Lord what that was, and the Lord spoke to me audibly and said, "That was a devil, and he just found out you woke up. When you wake up, it reverberates in the spirit realm, and the demons are notified that you are awake." I realized that I had become an enemy of satan. I had become a vital threat to the enemy because of what I know. When I tell people the truth, then it completely disarms the enemy from being able to attack them in the way that he has been able to.

It was enlightening to know that satan gets notified when we wake up and notified when we are praying in tongues. He knows if we are working and walking with God in a supernatural relationship. When we are yielding to the Spirit, it sends reverberations out into the spiritual realm, and demons know that. The demons know that there are sons and daughters of God who are walking the earth in understanding and authority, and there is nothing that they can do about it.

When the demons know that they can no longer get to you, they start working their way out to find a weak link in your life. They try to find someone else to enter into to get to you. They are always trying to find someone weaker to influence. As believers hear good teaching and more and more people hear the good news of the Gospel and grasp the truth, the circle keeps getting bigger. Before you know it, the body of Christ is being built up and unified, according to Ephesians 4. We start to see the unity in the faith, and the enemy cannot penetrate our borders.

You have to get to the place where you do not have a plan B because the devil does not have a plan B, and you make it work in your favor. You must be sold out, holy, set apart, and on fire with the holy fire of God from the altar of God. This is how we must live if we are going to receive from Heaven. You catch on fire and start burning. *"Who makes His angels spirits and His ministers a flame of fire"* (Heb. 1:7). Then the other realm starts to manifest because of who you are. You yield to that because you have been bought with a price.

> *Or do you not know that your body is the temple of the Holy Spirit who is in you, whom you have from God, and you are not your own? For you were bought at a price; therefore glorify God in your body and in your spirit, which are God's.*
>
> —1 Corinthians 6:19-20

Your body and your life are not your own anymore. Paul said it was as though Christ, who was inside of him, was borrowing his body daily. Jesus was living through Paul, and Paul became the expression of God. Paul had caught it. What if you could not fail? What if dying is a promotion? Because it is, and in realizing that you learn to live.

Your body and your life are
not your own anymore.

*And the Word became flesh and dwelt among us,
and we beheld His glory, the glory as of the only
begotten of the Father, full of grace and truth.*

—JOHN 1:14

The Trinity—the Father, the Son, and the Holy Spirit—
existed before the earth was formed. Jesus was pre-existent,
and then He was wrapped in flesh and "tabernacled" among
us. Every time a demon would recognize Him as the Son
of God, He would tell the demon to be quiet because Jesus
wanted to be known as the Son of Man. Jesus' mission was
to redeem man, so He did everything in the flesh as the Son
of Man and not the Son of God. That was why Jesus could
say, "The works that I am doing, you will also do and even
greater works" (see John 14:12). Jesus was keeping it within
the parameter of the son of man.

When satan tested Jesus in the desert, satan was trying to
get Jesus out of His parameter as the son of man. The tempter
said, *"If you are the Son of God, command these stones to become*

bread" (Matt. 4:3). The enemy was trying to get Jesus to act outside of His mission. Jesus came right back at satan with the Word of God. Jesus would not throw Himself off the temple because He could see that satan was trying to disqualify Him. Jesus came to redeem us because He is the Son of God, but He also came to show us how we are supposed to be living on this earth. Jesus stopped the devil from revealing who He was because He wanted people to see Him in the manifestation of the Father through the flesh as our example.

I beat up the devil every day. When I get up, I start praying in tongues, and I start calling on the fire from the altar. I call on my angels, and I say, "Open the books and whatever it says, then do it, Lord. I want Your books to be open before You, and whatever it says, I agree with You. Lord, I am going to do Your will today." Then I am led by the Spirit of God. Not driven but *led* by the Spirit of God. Whenever I choose to say something, I have a choice whether to yield to the Spirit or yield to myself. If I speak from the Spirit, then forever, there will be people changed. You must establish the authority that has been given to you in this earthly realm.

I went to Puerto Rico recently, and God told me to teach the people how to come against hurricanes and how to prosper. It did not surprise me that the demonic storm Dorian came by. When do you realize it is not a coincidence anymore, but it is just warfare? When do you start to realize that if this worked for Jesus and He told us it works for us, then you should not back off?

What did Jesus do? Jesus took authority over the storms, and He took authority over death. In the same breath, Jesus said, "Those believing ones will do these things in My name" (see Mark 16:17-18). He told them that they would raise the dead, heal the sick, and cast out devils. None of them is harder than the other because none of it is from you. It has to do with your authority because of ownership, because of holiness; you are set apart and holy under God as a holy nation. The authority that has been given to you is because you have been bought. You are part of the family. According to Romans 8:15, you have the spirit of adoption. The spirit of *acceptance* is what it says in Aramaic. You have the Spirit of God inside of you, saying, "Father, Father." You are adopted in, and you are accepted in the beloved.

THE WORD TRANSFORMS YOUR MIND

And do not be conformed to this world, but be transformed by the renewing of your mind, that you may prove what is that good and acceptable and perfect will of God.

—ROMANS 12:2

God has this amazing transforming power in the renewing of your mind by the Word of God. It has to do with your psychological makeup. It is dealing with the psychological realm that is attached to the physical realm. In First Thessalonians 5:23, Paul talks about your spirit, soul, and body and differentiates between the three parts of you. Your spirit is saved by the born-again experience but not your "soul" or "psyche," which is your mind. As a result of your mind not being born again, it must be transformed by the renewing of your mind by the Word of God. It is the Word of God that has to change your mind, change your will, and remove incorrect filters allowing you to catch God's truths as they come in so you may receive from Heaven.

You have to establish your authority by what you know in the Word of God. I have to back up what I say with Scripture. When I say something, I confirm it and seal it up, and we go on building precept upon precept. Your mind will withstand you, and people and demons know if you doubt. You have to be fully convinced not just in your spirit but in your soul.

You have to be transformed by the renewing of your mind that *you* may prove what the good and acceptable and perfect will of God is. There is a transformation that happens through the Word of God, and you are changed. Then you can look at anything and say whether it is acceptable. You can discern the perfect will of God, and then you can make decisions. You are in authority because you are under authority, and you can make just judgments. Your mind needs to be transformed.

> *For the weapons of our warfare are not carnal but mighty in God for pulling down strongholds, casting down arguments and every high thing that exalts itself against the knowledge of God,*

bringing every thought into captivity to the obedi-
ence of Christ.

—2 CORINTHIANS 10:4-5

You have to come against anything that comes against the knowledge of God. You have to bring every *thought* into captivity. This scripture is addressing spiritual warfare in your thought life. The word "thought" here is the word "psyche." If you get the psychological part of your mind in tune and on the same track as your spirit, then you can tell your body to take the day off. This will cause you to have authority over your body. It will not be long before you are skipping dessert to go exercise. Unless you can get your mind, will, and emotions (the psyche part of you) to form a coalition with your born-again spirit, you are going to get beat up. That is why so many feel trapped in a body. Allow the Word of God to transform your thinking and change your thought process.

God is Spirit, and those who worship Him must
worship in spirit and truth.

—JOHN 4:24

If you remember, Jesus here was talking to the Samaritan woman at the well. She wanted to talk to Jesus about theological perceptions among the people. Samaritans were considered half-breeds, and they had actually built a temple like the one in Jerusalem and were trying to set up their own traditions. They were arguing with the Israelites about which mountain they were supposed to worship on. The woman started arguing with Jesus, and He said, "Woman, the hour is coming when we will not worship on this mountain or any other mountain" (see John 4:21). Jesus confronted her, and He does that a lot with us. Like when believers think that the warfare they are going through is from God. Jesus confronts our misconceptions. Jesus was telling her that the mountain is not the issue because God is a Spirit, and He is going to accept spiritual worship. God is not going to talk to you through your mind or body. He is going to talk to you through the Spirit because He is a Spirit. God does not have to operate in the realm of the flesh.

God is not going to talk to you through your mind or body. He is going to talk to you through the Spirit because He is a Spirit.

You need to be transformed by the renewing of your mind, and you need to discipline your body daily. Paul said, *"But I keep under my body, and bring it into subjection: lest that by any means, when I have preached to others, I myself should be a castaway"* (1 Cor. 9:27 KJV). Paul would not let his body rule him because it would disqualify him as an apostle. We see ministers falling all the time today, but in this world none of us are immune. It has to do with the responsibility that God puts on us to discipline our own body and to renew our minds. A true spiritual person is not someone who is trying to be spiritual, but one who yields to the Holy Spirit. It is someone who has been given permission to be spiritual in all situations and still walks in the flesh on this earth as Jesus did.

THE PARABLE OF THE SOILS

The parable of the soils is very important in understanding how to receive from Heaven. In the parable, Jesus was sitting by the sea and speaking to a large crowd and told them the parable of the sower (see Mark 4:1-20). His disciples came to Him afterward and asked Him to explain it to them. Jesus told them that the sower sows the Word of God; the seed is the Word. The seed is not money; it is the Word of God. Jesus only spent one sentence of the parable on the seed and one on the sower, which represents the farmer. Jesus then spent paragraphs talking about the soil. Many people have called it the parable of the sower, but Jesus told me that He called it the parable of the soils.

Jesus explained that the soils represent the condition of men's hearts. Only one condition of the heart produced a harvest. Out of that one good soil condition that did produce, some had a 30-fold return, some a 60-fold return, and some a 100-fold return. Even out of the good soil, not everyone got a 100-fold return. Using simple math gives value to each of the four soils at 25 percent. Then according to the parable, out of

100 people receiving the Word, only 25 people out of the 100 will have the good soil to receive it.

Out of the 25 people who had good soil to receive the Word, you must now divide by three because their return was 30, 60, and 100-fold. So approximately eight people had a 30-fold return, eight people had a 60-fold return, and only eight people had a 100-fold return. Out of 100 people who hear the Word of God, only eight people will have a 100-fold return on it. Jesus then told His disciples that if they understood this, then they will know the deep secrets of the kingdom; then, they can understand everything. The Word of God transforms you and changes you because it is an impartation from Heaven.

If you want to know the deep secrets of what Jesus is saying to you in your heart, then you have to get rid of anything that is hindering you from that coming to pass. This means that for you to receive the Word of God, you must tend to the condition of your heart to make it optimal for growth. Once you do that, Jesus will be smiling at you. When satan was coming to Jesus, He said, "The evil one is coming, and he has nothing in me" (see John 14:30). The ruler of this world had nothing in Jesus' flesh to hook Him with, and that is what you should want.

SPEAKING THE MYSTERIES OF THE SPIRIT

For he who speaks in a tongue does not speak to men but to God, for no one understands him; however, in the spirit he speaks mysteries.

—1 CORINTHIANS 14:2

There are times when you have done everything you can do, and you still have not broken through. All of a sudden, at that very point of weakness, the Holy Spirit will come in, and He will lift you up, and you can pray in tongues with fire as you have never prayed before. We need to go to the next level because change has to occur, and change occurs in you first, and then it occurs in everything around you. Your body is flesh and blood. When you pray in the Spirit, in tongues, your body and mind do not participate because it is spiritual. When you sense the Holy Spirit, your mind cannot comprehend it; it happens inside of your heart. You need to turn your mind off and start focusing on the Word of God.

If you pray in the Spirit and truly connect with the Holy Spirit, you send out a reverberation in the Spirit; I saw this when I was in Heaven. The Lord Jesus said to me, "Pray in the Spirit right now." I was thinking, "Really?" My body is on the operating table, and I am in the spirit. Jesus said again, "Pray, pray, pray!" I did, and there was power that went out from me and started hitting things!

Change occurs in you
first, and then it occurs in
everything around you.

We recently took over another part of the building where we have our offices to make a second studio because we are growing. We installed security cameras, and I had them hooked up to the infrared camera on my phone. That night we turned off the lights in the studio and headed back to our offices. From the office, I could see on my phone that there were demons in the studio, and we were catching them on film with the cameras! I showed Kathi the phone and said, "Let's start praying in tongues." We were in the other office on the other side of the building. As soon as we started praying in tongues, the demons started scattering. We went over there and started pleading the blood of Jesus and "beating up" the demons, casting them all out.

You have to establish your authority in the realm of the Spirit. God has given you authority, but you have to establish it; you have to make yourself known. It is like a GPS signal in the spirit realm, and you have to send out a signal and then you are established in the Spirit in your area. You do not want yourself or anyone you know harassed by the demonic, so you must take your authority in Jesus' name.

Whether you see Jesus on earth or you do not see Jesus until you die, you are going to have to confront the devil. Demons do not get it unless you are rough with them. The devil should not be enjoying church, and he should not be sitting on the front row, saying, "Hey, they are playing my favorite song. I hope he talks about how God loves everyone, no matter what they do, and that there is no problem with you living with your girlfriend."

At one of our meetings, a young woman asked me for prayer, and she told me she had female problems. I asked her, "Are you married?" She said, "No, I'm not really into that. I live with my boyfriend, and you know we are just not into that marriage thing." She is not going to get healed. "Narrow is the way, and few find it" (see Matt. 7:13-14). You have to repent of any sin in your life. You have to be covered in the blood of Jesus and repent right now. People are dating the devil during the week and going to church on the weekends.

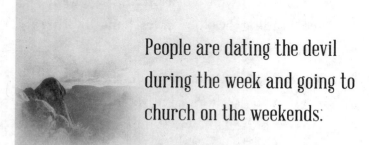

People are dating the devil during the week and going to church on the weekends.

You think you want Jesus to visit you, but you might want to reconsider. You think you want Him to speak at your church, but you might want to reconsider that too because He may just unload on everyone. Jesus said, "Unless you drink My blood and eat My flesh, you will have no part in Me" (see John 6:53). When Jesus said that many people left Him that day, and Jesus turned a very large crowd into a small Bible study! Jesus thinned out His disciples to twelve. Jesus was, in essence, saying that the thousands following Him were there because of the miracles they saw and because they were fed. They were not interested in following God. The best thing you can do is pray with fire and repent daily.

THE GLORY OF HIS FACE

Jesus has made an open show of the devil. Jesus Christ triumphed over him, embarrassed him, and put His foot on the devil's head and took him out. Death has no power over you as a Christian because death is a promotion, and there is no loss. You are not to be afraid of death any longer. Jesus spoke to me at length about Psalm 91, which was written by Moses. Moses composed the whole Psalm while he was trying to stay alive in the cleft of the rock because God had simply walked by him (see Exod. 33:22). God was announcing His goodness and His name to Moses, and Moses was seeing God in multiple ways at once.

God said, "You know what Moses? Me and you are fine; it is those people, your people." Moses said, "No, they are Your people." God replied, "Excuse Me. When did they become My people?" (see Exod. 32:7-14). Moses knew they were done for if God got mad at the people. Moses wanted to remind God that they were God's people in order to protect them. God said to Moses, "I am pleased with you. My presence shall go with you." What is interesting is there is no word in Hebrew for *presence*. The word they use is *face*. But when God said to Moses that His "presence" would go with him, God used the plural Hebrew word *faces*. Moses had a revelation of the Holy Trinity. Then Moses asked God to show him His glory. God told Moses that he could not see God's face and live, and they worked out a way for that to happen (see Exod. 33:18-23).

You cannot see the face of God and live. I was not allowed to look at the face of the Father when I was in Heaven, but I could stare at Jesus all day. What was coming out of the face of the Father would not allow me to come back to my body because my body would melt. You cannot see the face of the Father and live down here, and that is what God said. Your body cannot handle it because it is fallen.

So, if you are not living right, you need to fix that first, and you need to repent. If you repent, the demons will come but will not be able to do anything. Then they will find someone else who is weak, and they will go after them because they work on commission. Demons need to have results, or they get in trouble. You have to repent, and you turn your face toward God, and that is His presence; it is His face. And that is the glory, which is coming, and you must be ready to receive it.

When I was in Heaven, I had an encounter and was taken to a place, and the Lord told me that not everyone would get to see this. Recently the same thing happened in our living room at home, and I experienced it again. Kathi asked me, "Whoa, what was that?" I said, "This is *that*." I could not put it into words. The Father came into our living room. The Father and the glory of God were so strong that Kathi and I sat there and stared at each other. There was so much love in that room. There was so much acceptance, there was so much of Heaven that nothing mattered anymore, and everything inside of me was activated.

This glory is what is coming to the church, and it is what removes the spots and wrinkles from the bride's dress. It is starting now, and it does not involve laying on of hands, prophecy, or offerings. It involves people who have repented and prepared themselves and their oil lamps for the bridegroom (see Matt. 25:1-13). You are being groomed for marriage. The glory is going to come in now, and it is the weighty presence of God, the *kabod* of God. It is not what you are used to experiencing. In the glory, you will get healed immediately, and you will hear from God immediately. I have already seen it.

I was taken to the future, and I saw in the Spirit that there were churches everywhere with lines of people outside. People were waiting to get into the next service because they did not get into the first one. Those who were waiting were not saved, and they had heard that you would get healed if you could get into the building. I stood in line with people whose doctors had given up on them. I was caught up in the future, and I saw these end times.

The glory of the Lord was resting on the body of Christ, and the sons and daughters of God were being revealed, and the people of the world were flocking to God. They were coming and saying, "Please pray for me. I want God. I want to give my life to God." I was walking down the street, and people were calling out, "There is one of those sons of God; have him pray for us." All of the believers were recognized because their faces were glowing.

At the end of the age, we will become like Enoch. We will begin to walk over, and then one step later we will be gone, and that is what I saw. The church was a type of Enoch, and Enoch was a type of the church. I saw meetings where God was in charge, and we worshiped, and we preached, and we worshiped, and we preached, and people came in and were healed. You could hear bones cracking and joints going back together and people screaming because they got new limbs and new organs. Cancers were lying all over the floor. I saw people wanting to get saved because they wanted what we had. Can you imagine that?

OVERWHELMED BY THE OTHER REALM

For 30 years, I dealt with unsaved people at my job. Every day I talked to them about the Lord. They said, "Well, why should I give my life to Lord? What do you have that I don't have?" You know you could give them the standard answer and sell them the fire insurance that will keep them out of hell. But what if the goodness of God is what leads you to repentance (see Rom. 2:4)? What if God is so good that it leads people to repent and they want what you have? There is coming a time where the world will see the glory of God, and they will know that we are walking in the truth.

There is coming a time where the world will see the glory of God, and they will know that we are walking in the truth.

I am telling you this because right now, there is deception in the body of Christ. We are waiting for the white horse to come back, and He is not coming back until China, Russia, and the Middle East come in. Not to mention your neighbor coming in. He is the Lord of the harvest, and He is praying that people will *go out* into the harvest (see Matt. 9:38). You do not have to go very far because right now countries are coming to us. You do not have to go to Iran. I go to Iranian churches in the United States, and it does not take me two days to get there. It takes me a couple of hours, and I can preach to people in Farsi with a translator so they can hear the Gospel.

We are praying, but what we are praying for is that laborers would go into the harvest. Isaiah said, "Lord, send me," because he got touched by the other realm (see Isa. 6:1-8). Isaiah was a major prophet, and he got caught up, and saw the Lord, high and lifted up, and became undone. Everything was fine until the other realm influenced him. Isaiah touched that realm, and he said, "I am a man of unclean lips, and I am among a people of unclean lips." Isaiah was undone even though he was a major prophet. I'm sure he then saw himself as a minor prophet. His eyes had seen the King, the Lord of hosts. He started saying, "Woe is me." This kind of revelation is going to start happening everywhere.

Isaiah needed help, so an angel was sent to take a coal from the altar in Heaven that is burning right now. The angel put the burning coal right on Isaiah's lips and fixed it. Isaiah's response was, "Here I am! Send me!" Why? Isaiah had received something from the other realm that everyone else needed. You should not want to be normal. You should want to be an anomaly, a spike in the data that is unexplainable. You have to be touched from the other realm and be overwhelmed.

When I graduated from college, the head of my college spoke at the commencement ceremony. This is what he said: "Congratulations, you are going into the ministry. Just remember one thing. Jesus preached the will of the Father, and they killed Him in three and a half years. If you do the same, you will not last long either." He was making a point here. Did you ever notice that the people of times past who did anything for God are heroes now, but people wanted to kill them when they were alive? Jesus went and raised Lazarus from the dead and the religious leaders could not do anything about it. They could not stop Jesus, but they thought about how they were going to kill Lazarus because he was the evidence. The religious leaders of the day want to kill the evidence.

I have studied every known man and woman of God, and every move of God, and it took years. I found out what they did wrong, and I found out what they did right, and I learned from their mistakes. The one thing that I found is that they were not heroes in their generation. They were celebrated later, but at the time that they ministered, they made people feel uncomfortable because they preached repentance. They needed to move and be transformed and change and shift with what God was doing in their generation.

If I do not do my part in my generation, then a missing piece will be present and transferred over to the next generation.

If I do not do my part in my generation, then a missing piece will be present and transferred over to the next generation. If I do not tell you that we need to make course corrections now, the next generation will see it, identify it, and write about it. It happens all the time on Monday morning after watching a game the night before. Everybody can be better than the quarterback the following morning. Anyone can look back and say, "We should have done this, and you should have done that." How about if we make the course corrections now, and we end up going out with glory, and we complete our part of the race with excellence.

Everybody is an expert afterward. However, there are those who were in it before us, and who died in faith, fighting for what we believe in now. They paid a high price, and with that price is an investment. In Heaven right now, the cloud of witnesses is waiting for us to fulfill our part of the race. They already did their part, and they are cheering us on to the finish. I have met some of them. I did not meet them on the earth, but I met them in Heaven. I have had conversations with some of them for hours in earth time. When I was with Jesus, it was for a whole week, but it was only 45 minutes in earth time. I sat with evangelists you would know. They were so excited about what is next because they did their part, and now they are waiting for us to do our part. Do not find yourself behind the curve on what God is doing in your life because there are so many people who depend upon you to be faithful.

In Heaven right now, the cloud of witnesses is waiting for us to fulfill our part of the race. They already did their part, and they are cheering us on to the finish.

Jesus sometimes takes me in the spirit to show me things, and then He brings me back. One day He said, "Kevin, you know that I can bring you back five minutes before I came and got you?" I said, "You can do that?" Jesus said, "I can do anything I want. I can fix your past." I answered, "Really!" and He already has. The God you serve is not bound by any of the laws that you are bound by. God made the game, the board, and the pieces, and He always wins. It is His game, but He is not playing games with you. What God is doing is He is whispering in your ear and telling you that if you want to make history, then do not be normal. This generation does not need normal.

This generation does
not need normal.

Every generation needs the bar set higher. When you walk into a place, it should shift the atmosphere to where the devils that are occupying that place bail on you. When you sing songs, it should not be the devil's favorite song because it has no faith and Jesus' name is not in it. You should be doing things that shift atmospheres. Heroes are made for the next generation, but in this generation that you are in, you are going to have to discern how to mess with history. I mess with history and change it every day.

For instance, I get in there, and I mess up the plans of the enemy because a person was going to die and now they are not going to die.

The former company that I worked with, Southwest Airlines, used to send me my flight information a month ahead of time. I would have the tail number of the plane that I was assigned to and the names of all the employees who would be flying with me. My company knew exactly what was going to happen 30 days before it happened, and you do not think *God* is better than that? People would ask me, "Weren't you afraid you were going to crash?" You have got to be kidding me. If the mechanics knew the tail number that I was going to fly a month ahead of time, then God probably knew it a little bit more than that. Don't you think God can fix an airplane before it gets to me? Don't you think if I said, "Lord, I pray for the mechanics, that they do not miss a thing on that airplane," 30 days before I ever got on that plane, God would hear me? The mechanic might walk by and not even know why he looked at the wing a second time and noticed a crack. But I know why and it's because I am listening to my spirit, which is broadcasting that I shall live and not die (see Ps. 118:17).

I am not getting on a broken airplane, and I did four to six flights a day for 29 years and never went into the ground and never even had a sad story. How many of you have sat there and said, "I hope we don't crash"? You have to know that you can mess with the future as well as anything else in prayer by faith and by your relationship with God.

Abraham lived in Ur of the Chaldees when God called him (see Gen. 12:1-3). God visited Abraham and said, "I am going to make My covenant with you and make a nation out of you." God said, "Your name shall no longer be Abram, but Abraham, and I am going to make you the father of everyone" (see Gen. 17). That is what God does to each one of us when we are born again. I saw that by the faith of Abraham God could visit you and change the world with one visit. Abraham left for a city whose builder and maker was God (see Heb. 11:10). He did not know where he was going, but he would know when he got there.

By chapter 13 of Genesis, it says that Abraham was very rich. He left everything, and it did not take him long to prosper. Jesus said, "If you leave houses and families for My sake, and the Gospel's sake, will you not in this life receive a hundredfold, and persecutions as well?" (see Mark 10:29-30).

> *Just as Abraham "believed God, and it was accounted to him for righteousness." Therefore know that only those who are of faith are sons of Abraham. And the Scripture, foreseeing that God would justify the Gentiles by faith, preached the gospel to Abraham beforehand, saying, "In you all the nations shall be blessed." So then those who are of faith are blessed with believing Abraham.*
> —GALATIANS 3:6-9

Abraham followed God, and he became the father of us all. When we come to faith in Jesus Christ, we partake of the blessings of Abraham. We become sons of Abraham and receive his inheritance, and part of the blessing that is on Abraham is for changing a generation. It is our heritage and our inheritance through the covenant that God made with Abraham received through faith.

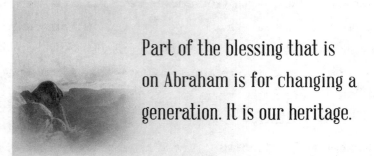

Part of the blessing that is on Abraham is for changing a generation. It is our heritage.

When are you going to let the Holy Spirit change a generation? When are you going to let Him shift you into what you already have inside of you? It comes through prayer, repentance, and humility. It comes through the crucified life, the fear of the Lord, and waiting on God. It comes through laying your life down and considering others more than yourself. There is a price that you pay, but God will quadruple it, and He will reward you. You cannot lose!

Chapter 4

RECEIVING FROM GOD

*Now may the God of peace Himself sanctify
you completely; and may your whole spirit,
soul, and body be preserved blameless at
the coming of our Lord Jesus Christ.*

—1 THESSALONIANS 5:23

EVERY PERSON IS MADE UP OF THREE PARTS. YOU
have a spirit, a soul—*your mind, will, and emotions*—
and a body. These different parts used to operate in
unity before the fall, but now they are separate. You are very
complicated, and to understand other realms you must first
understand yourself. You were built to operate at very high
efficiency in the Spirit, where all the realms work together.

Now that man has fallen, you are trapped inside of a body that wants to do its own thing, and you have a mind that wants to do its own thing. The problem is that once you are born again, your spirit wants to do God's thing.

The apostle Paul wrote chapter seven of the book of Romans to explain what happens to a saved person living in this earthly realm. However, when he switches from chapter seven over to chapter eight, Paul says, *"There is therefore now no condemnation* [there's no accusing voice] *to those who are in Christ Jesus."* Your case has "been closed" is what it says in Aramaic. He continues by teaching that *"to those who are in Christ Jesus, who do not walk according to the flesh, but according to the Spirit."* Paul explains that those who live by the Spirit please God, but those who live by the flesh cannot please God.

> *Therefore, if anyone is in Christ, he is a new creation; old things have passed away; behold, all things have become new.*
> —2 Corinthians 5:17

If you are born again, and you have given yourself over to the Lord and the Spirit of God is in you, then you are a new creature. Paul is telling the Corinthians that they are a completely new species, and there is nothing like you. You are all new, and everything old has passed away. Romans 7 is what happens when you yield to the flesh and when you yield to your mind because it wants to go its own way, and then you cannot please God. Romans seven is where you live if you have not allowed God to take over your life and become yielded to Him, whereas chapter eight brings you into the Spirit realm where you become more than a conqueror through Him who loved you (see Rom. 8:37).

You must walk a disciplined life down here, and you have to keep your edge. You must always be alert, and you have got to be on your game. It is not that hard even though it seems that way at first because you are fighting devils all the time in the Spirit. People have asked me, "Is there really a devil behind every tree?" I always say, "No, there are five, so I take out the tree as well."

The devils are packed in down here on the earth. When I was in Heaven, the Lord turned me around and let me look at the earth from Heaven's perspective. I could see everything, and I understood in a flash what was going on here on earth, and that is why I said, "I am not going back." You need to be ready for what you are really dealing with down here. I saw that the demonic spirits here know that they are done for and that they can never be redeemed. They are disembodied, and they seek embodiment because they want expression, and they want to get back at God. When God flooded the earth in Noah's time, all of those spirits of the hybrids were disembodied, and there is no redemption for them. They are wreaking havoc down here, and that is why the weapons of our warfare are not carnal (see 2 Cor. 10:4-6).

DOMINIONS AND DOMAINS

We are not warring against human beings but different high classes of spirits. There are different levels of demon spirits, and some of them are a hybrid of animals and humans. You need to get bold because you are dealing with devils that hate God and hate you. You need to turn the tables on them and make *them* miserable and remind them of their demise. Remind them that you are in, and they are out and that you are the head, so you are in charge. You have to tell those devils what to do and not let them tell *you* what to do.

You need to get bold because you are dealing with devils that hate God and hate you. You need to turn the tables on them and make *them* miserable and remind them of their demise.

The way that you deal with the demonic is by your understanding that you have three parts, and the devil will never win in the spirit. He will win in your soul or your body if you let him, so never let him in. Despite that, the devil will never be able to get into your spirit because the Holy Spirit would annihilate him. The Holy Spirit will not allow you to be possessed in your spirit, but your soul and your body can be attacked. That is why you have to transform your mind by the Word of God. It has nothing to do with possession but has everything to do with dominions and domains. How much right have you given the devil over your kingdom? How much have you truly turned over to the Lord Jesus Christ? That is why you need to side with God's Word in your mind and in your body. Romans 7 should not be happening in your life. You should not be warring within yourself.

People let the war get in them. You cannot receive from God if you do not understand what I am saying here. Receiving from God has to do with you completely yielding all your members. Everything about you has to be yielded to God and be continually submitted to God's will. That means that you do not do what you want to do. If you have settled in your mind that you are not going to go there, then do not let your mind think about it. If it is trespassing, then do not do it.

If you have settled in your mind that you are not going to go there, then do not let your mind think about it. If it is trespassing, then do not do it.

*I was in the Spirit on the Lord's Day, and I heard
behind me a loud voice, as of a trumpet, saying, "I
am the Alpha and the Omega, the First and the
Last."*

—REVELATION 1:10-11

Jesus started this, and He is going to end it, as He is, *"the
author and the finisher of* [our] *faith"* (Heb. 12:2), who is framing your world by His Word. According to Zephaniah 3:17,
the Lord is a mighty warrior who is singing songs of deliverance over you. Jeremiah 29:11 lets you know that the Lord
plans to prosper you and that He has a good and expected end
planned for you.

*Trust in the Lord with all your heart, and lean
not on your own understanding; in all your ways
acknowledge Him, and He shall direct your paths.*

—PROVERBS 3:5-6

Learn to acknowledge God in everything. Always
acknowledge the Lord, and do not lean on your own understanding. I wait for the Lord to explain Himself, and if He
does not, I do not question it. Everybody is in a big hurry to
resolve things. Some things are none of your business, and
you may never know what happened or why it happened. I
have walked away from things and said, "Lord, I may never
know what just happened there, but it is fine with me." I have
got to be who I am supposed to be. I cannot let people disqualify me. My spiritual father says that if you get offended,

you become just like those who offend. Do you want to be just like them because they are neutralizing you? He says that you can get hurt, but you should never get offended because you do not want to be knocked out of the race.

When God speaks to you, He is going to speak to you through the still small voice in your spirit. If there is a lot of noise going on in your soul, you will experience it in your mind, will, and emotions. There is also noise in the physical realm that you experience with your body. This noise comes to distract and causes you to have a hard time discerning God's voice even though it is very loud.

> You can get hurt, but you should never get offended because you do not want to be knocked out of the race.

FIND YOURSELF IN THE WORD

Daniel was a prophet who was in a really bad situation. He lived about 400 years before Jesus came. Daniel was all set up in Jerusalem, and suddenly another country came in and took them as captives, and it was not in his plan. Daniel was in Babylon after 70 years, and he had a scroll that the prophet

Jeremiah wrote years before. Daniel was reading and got to chapter 29, and it said, "You will be carried into captivity, but at the end of seventy years, you will cry out to Me, and I will hear you and deliver you back into the land because I have a good plan for you. Plans for you to prosper and have an expected end" (see Jer. 29:10-12). Can you imagine being in captivity for 70 years, opening your Bible to read, and you suddenly find yourself in there? Can you imagine what that was like?

The Lord Jesus Christ showed me this, and He sent me back from the dead to tell you that it is rigged in your favor. It is already written down in Heaven. All of a sudden, as Daniel is reading the scroll, this scenario unfolds, and he is in there. The scroll told Daniel to cry out to God, so he cried out and began to pray and fast, but it was already rigged in his favor. God framed Daniel's world before he was born.

Daniel believed that he could pray for this deliverance, but then he prayed, and nothing happened for 21 days. After the 21 days, an angel came and told Daniel that God had heard him on the first day that he prayed, but that they had been fighting in the heavenlies to get to him. God began to open the spirit realm to Daniel, and he was taken and shown all those things that were coming. He was able to understand what was going on in the world at that time. He was able to see all the world powers that rose after him, and he got to see many events before they happened. Jesus came to die for you and save your life, but you need to implement it into your life. You need to find yourself in the Bible. You are seated with

Him in the heavenly places far above all rule and authority (see Eph. 1:21; 2:6).

Daniel became a mighty prophet of God, and he got to see things that we do not even know about. Daniel was told not to tell anyone what the seven thunders said, and he was told to seal the book up until the end time (see Dan. 12:4). Daniel was in captivity when he read Jeremiah's scroll, but things changed within 24 hours and then 21 days. All of the captives came back with Daniel to Israel, and then Jesus the Messiah came, and they were right in their place. You are right where God wants you. The angels of the Lord will escort you into the perfect will of God because that is what they do, but what they need from you is some cooperation. When I talk to angels, I tell them that I am all in with them, and I tell them that I do not know everything but they do so let's just do this.

God is framing your world right now, and you are being set up for the supernatural. When you became born again, you became a supernatural being, and you became an enemy of the devil. You never had to say or do anything to cause the demons to hate you; it was just that you chose sides. You need to get over it, and you need to make a difference in this generation by grasping the fact that you are in three parts down here. You need to receive from God in your spirit, but you need to let your mind and your body behave so that you do not become disqualified.

> *But the natural man does not receive the things of the Spirit of God, for they are foolishness to him; nor can he know them, because they are spiritually*

discerned. But he who is spiritual judges all things,
yet he himself is rightly judged by no one.

—1 CORINTHIANS 2:14-15

This verse will explain some things to you. You are a spirit in a body, and you have a soul (which is your mind, will, and emotions). In your spirit, you can discern spiritual things, but your mind does not comprehend them. That is why when you get baptized in the Holy Spirit and you pray in tongues, your mind does not participate. Paul says, *"If I pray in a tongue, my spirit prays, but my understanding is unfruitful"* (1 Cor. 14:14). Because you are praying out mysteries in your spirit, you are speaking to God in your spirit, and your mind does not comprehend it. Your mind is not part of the process. If your understanding is from your mind, will, and emotions instead of from your spirit, you will misinterpret what God is saying and doing.

You should block off an hour a day to pray in tongues if possible. Do you say that you cannot do that? Well, enjoy your life because you have just settled for the natural man. The spirit man needs to pray in tongues. Your spirit man has already scheduled you to pray in tongues every day. My wife and I sometimes pray 14-hour days in tongues, and we like it. Please do not do that if you are not supposed to do that. We do it because we like to do it, and the Spirit of God is so intoxicating, and this is how I fight my battles.

The spirit man needs to pray in tongues.

If any man speak, let him speak as the oracles of God; if any man minister, let him do it as of the ability which God giveth: that God in all things may be glorified through Jesus Christ, to whom be praise and dominion for ever and ever. Amen.

—1 PETER 4:11 KJV

You have a spiritual supply from Heaven, and you must administer it with the ability that God supplies to you. You must learn how to transfer and take that which is from the spiritual realm and bring it into the physical realm. When you give out what you have received from Heaven as an ambassador to the kingdom, God gets the glory. God is recognized in His domain when you are doing the will of your heavenly Father on earth. Let the Holy Spirit help you to interpret correctly and implement the will of God in your life

But I say to you that for every idle word men may speak, they will give account of it in the day of

judgment. For by your words you will be justified,
and by your words you will be condemned.

—MATTHEW 12:36-37

Jesus was teaching that you will be held accountable for every idle word that comes out of your mouth. Jesus told me in person that I am going to be held accountable for every idle word that comes out of my mouth. I saw that this truth is not restrictive, but rather it is empowering because my words have greater weight when I do not waste them or use them idly. Now when I say what I mean and I mean what I say, I notice that there is an edge about me in the spirit and I receive from Heaven. Doors are opened for me when I speak, I hear them open, I hear things break, and I hear chains falling off.

SPEAK FROM THE OTHER REALM

I can speak from the other realm, and it influences a room. We are supposed to be living in this kind of authority. I do not claim to be anyone special; any one of you could do this. Jesus told me to work myself out of a job, training everyone to walk in His authority. When you do not need me anymore, that is just fine, and it would be my dream. I want you to be better than me. I do not care that you get more attention than I do because I do not want the attention. That is why I am in the position I am in, because if you yield to the Spirit you will be taken to the front of the line, you will be given a place to speak. You will be given a place to shift atmospheres and shift a generation back to God.

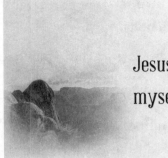

Jesus told me to work myself out of a job.

You can shift a generation; you can do it. John the Baptist did it, the widow with two mites did it, and Mary did it. Look at the mothers who were visited by angels when they became pregnant in Scripture, and the angels told them about the baby that was in their womb. The God I serve says that He speaks those things that are not as though they were (see Rom. 4:17). What is in you that has not come out yet is just as real as when it does happen. You are a history maker, and you do not have to hand off the baton to another generation and give them a bad position in the race when you are yielded to God.

I used to run on the track team when I was in school. One day after racing all day, my track coach told me a runner had dropped out of the next relay race. He asked me if I could be the anchor for the two-mile relay. He said we had a chance to break the state record. I explained to him that I had just run three races and could not possibly help him. He insisted and advised me, "Just run as though somebody is trying to chase and kill you." I was a long-distance runner, but the coach explained that he just needed a warm body.

So, I did it, but they had to train me to grab the baton in a certain way as my teammate passed it off to me. I had to be up to speed between marks on the track as he came flying by, and I needed to avoid passing over certain lines. Mike said, "He is going to put it right in your hand, and as soon as you feel it, grab it, but do not look back and do not stop until you win."

I got ready and watched as the first runner fell behind, then the second runner had fallen even further behind. It was at the end of the race, and I was handed the baton. Mathematically I was looking at this, and it seemed impossible. You do not want to do that to another generation. I ran that leg, and when they timed me, I had run a quarter mile in 52.6 seconds, which was the school record for the quarter mile. We had won the state record!

In a relay race, every leg counts toward the end result. We must do our part in this generation. What satan does not understand or expect is that when he decides to harass and provoke you, you are pushed into the glory. The devil has done you a favor because that is when you come to the end of yourself. He pushes you into the glory, and in the glory there is favor and favor is not fair.

Someone has to let God move them, and then they move a generation. There are prophets in this land who need to speak, and there are apostles who need to plant. There are evangelists who need to preach the uncompromised Word of God. There are teachers who need to teach doctrine, solid doctrine, and there are pastors who need to stay in their post and shepherd people. We need all of them.

Someone has to let God move them, and then they move a generation.

> *For the word of God is living and powerful, and sharper than any two-edged sword, piercing even to the division of soul and spirit, and of joints and marrow, and is a discerner of the thoughts and intents of the heart.*
> —HEBREWS 4:12

People have made Jesus someone He is not. Jesus has a two-edged sword, and one side is to cut you, and one is to cut the enemy. The Word of God divides between the soul and the spirit. Some believers have to apologize to Ananias and Sapphira because they have done worse than this couple did. Ananias and Sapphira died in the New Covenant, in grace.

When I was 19 years old, Jesus told me to stop pursuing my admission to the Air Force Academy because I was going to go to a Bible college instead. He told me that I was going to become a minister of the Gospel. Jesus appeared to me, and He said, "Kevin, you are going to go to this college and get your education, and then you are going to work for an airline as a career." I was 25 years old when I was hired at an airline after completing seven years of college.

Jesus had told me that the reason for my career was so that my message would never be manipulated by money. I would have a career and retire and go into ministry. For 30 years, I was employed by Southwest Airlines, and I thought I was going to be a pilot. Jesus told me, "No, you are going to be a flight attendant." I said, "What?" But when Jesus was done with me, I was done with the world because He had conquered me. I am going to say whatever the Lord has me say, and I will never compromise.

THE LIMITATION FALLACY

The apostle Paul said, *"Have I therefore become your enemy because I tell you the truth?"* (Gal. 4:16). The reason why you are experiencing the war that you are going through is that you do not understand what is going on around you. If you did, you would no longer experience demonic activity in your life. The devil knows when you know your authority in Christ Jesus, and he backs off.

I saw that my whole life was based on fear, and when I met Jesus the love that was in His eyes came into me and drove out fear. I became perfected in His love. I saw that Jesus believed in me, and He told me that all of Heaven is behind me. Everyone in Heaven loves us and talks about us, and they will never limit us. No one in Heaven thinks we are going to fail, and they are for us.

If you can get rid of fear and be perfected in His love, then you can do anything that God says that you can do. The limits have been taken off. I came back from the dead to tell you that it is fake news down here. It is being broadcast all the time, and it is telling you what you cannot do. There must be a turn in your life, a shift that causes you to become the lender and not the borrower. A point has to come when you become the head and not the tail, and where you have a command about you and people know that God is with you (see Deut. 28:12-13). There is overcoming power in the blood of Jesus. There is overcoming power in the name of Jesus.

You begin to realize that you have been wronged, and the atmosphere of Heaven is available. Jesus told me that if I go back for Him, I cannot lose. What does that consist of, and what does that mean? In the very fabric of who God is, He has never once thought of failure, and He has never once thought of rejection. He sits on His throne, and He is waiting for His enemies to be made His footstool (see Heb. 10:13). God trusts you so much that He told Jesus, on the way out of the grave, to hand over the keys to the church. *"I will build my church, and the gates of hell shall not prevail against it. I will give you the keys of the kingdom of heaven"* (Matt. 16:18-19 ESV). God needs brave *sent ones* who are not doing it for themselves but for the kingdom of God, in order to please God. When you get someone down here who agrees with God, they are unstoppable.

God trusts you so much that He told Jesus, on the way out of the grave, to hand over the keys to the church.

The Lord Himself, before you were born, approved of you. In Heaven, when I looked into Jesus' eyes, He said, "Kevin, I remember the day, when I thought of you. I named you, and I spoke you into your mother's womb," and He smiled at me. Jesus said, "You turned out just like I thought of you." He told me not to hold back and to tell everyone how much God loves people. He told me to tell everyone that what they have heard about Jesus is not always correct. He is not weak; He is a very strong Commander, and He loves you, and He has gone to war for you.

When I was in Rome, Italy, I was at the place where Paul had been held prisoner and eventually was beheaded. The original Roman streets of stone are still there. They showed me where Paul was beheaded, and they took me down to his holding cell. I could not stand up in that cell, and they still had chains there that were about a meter long. While I was there, God spoke to me, and I had a visitation. The Father said to me, "Paul chose to write from his revelation in that cell, instead of his circumstances, and because of that, you now benefit from his choice." He said, "You do the same thing, and do not speak from your circumstances. You preach the uncompromised Word of God. You change a generation; you change history." You see how God has not put limitations on you? You need to absorb this important truth to help you to become a good receiver from Heaven.

Paul changed history because he chose not to write from his circumstances. If you saw the conditions that he was subjected to, you would understand, and yet Paul considered himself a happy man and said, "I take hold of that which Christ has taken hold of for me" (see Phil. 3:12-14). Then Paul wrote his letters to the churches, and he lost his head. He said, "Don't worry about me because there is a crown laid up for me and to all who have loved His appearing" (see 2 Tim. 4:8).

THE TRUTH ABOUT DEMONIC INFLUENCE OVER YOUR PERSONALITY

I received my bachelor's degree at a particular Bible college, and later the Lord sent me to another Bible training center. However, I learned that we cannot get so locked into a certain way of thinking and doctrine that we forget that God is also above and beyond even positive thinking or positive speech. Jesus appeared to me when I died on the operating table. I met Him in person, and spent time with Him. I found out that He is not tied to any denomination, and He is not Word of Faith; He is *I Am*. He is the center of the universe.

Jesus is not tied to any denomination, and He is not Word of Faith; He is *I Am.* He is the center of the universe.

In that realm, standing there with the Lord for forty-five minutes, I started to get to know Him a little better. I noticed that Jesus does have a personality, and I was given a revelation about personalities that the Lord told me to share. I realized that we often say, "Well, that's just Sally," or "You know that's just Jim," but it is not. A lot of what you think is a personality is actually demonic activity.

I have a friend who prays in tongues a lot, and when he walks into a room devils begin leaving people. However, he could not find anyone to deliver him when he had devils of oppression. He went from pastor to pastor, and they said, "Well, you are a Christian so you cannot have devils." He said, "Well, you tell *them* that because I am in bondage, and I cannot break free." This man is my friend, and it took him a year, but he said he finally cast out many devils away from himself. Now, when you listen to a CD of his, you can begin sensing oppression leaving you, even if you don't believe in that.

When I was with Jesus, I realized that His personality, the way He is as a person, completely matches His Word.

Whatever Jesus says is who He is, and so He keeps His Word. Jesus' personality is contagious, and He is very forthright, and He knows what He wants. You do not walk away from Him wondering what He was trying to tell you; you *know* what He was saying to you. Wouldn't it be nice to have a group of friends like that and a church that operates that way? A place where you can get together, and you do not work against each other. Where you agree with each other, and it affects your town or your neighborhood in your city. This is the kind of personality that I believe Jesus Christ imparted to us.

> *Therefore become imitators of God [copy Him and follow His example], as well-beloved children [imitate their father].*
> —EPHESIANS 5:1 AMP

Paul clearly tells us to be imitators of God. As children, we imitate our father. What you will find in the next few weeks is that God is going to start showing you the parts of your personality that have been influenced by demonic activity. That does not mean you are possessed. There are dominions and domains, and demons can work in close proximity to you to try and influence you to take on their way of thinking. They do not have to possess you, throw you down, and cause you to foam at the mouth. They influence your thinking and try to convince you that you are something that you are not. You may start to act the way that they are telling you to because of the influence in your thought processes, and it is completely demonic, but you think it is you.

I have to tell you these things because it is what I saw on the other side. Jesus took me to a restaurant, and all the people were seated there at tables of two or four, and it was full. I looked, and every single person in that restaurant had a demon entity standing beside them. The closer the demon was allowed to be to a person, the more the person started to look like that entity. Those people even started to have the same hand motions and the characteristics of their demon. They started to look like puppets, and I saw that as the demons motioned, their assigned person would begin to copy the same motions. It was bizarre. I saw that the demons were trying to work themselves into their people's bodies and minds. The demons do not want you to know this kind of thing.

When I was with Jesus, I saw that my personality had to be based on the original record and the original architect's plans for me. I do not cease to be Kevin by that happening, but I become the Kevin who is not consistently 20 minutes late or the Kevin who does not lie. You should not say, "Well, that's just Charlie. He is always late." No, Charlie is not supposed to be late, and he is not supposed to lie to me or steal from me.

At Southwest Airlines, where I worked, you did not steal or tell lies about your time at work, and if you did you were fired. If you were 30 seconds late, you got fined $1,200, and if you did it three times, you were fired. Many employees disappeared, and they were all good people, but, "Oh, that's just Sally," did not cut it. It does not work when 175 people are waiting on an airplane for Sally to show up to work. It is not just your personality; sometimes it can be demonic activity. It can be an attack against you to keep you late, to keep you frustrated. Stuff piles up, and all you want to do is get to your car. Everything is unleashed against you to show you that you are a loser and that you cannot do anything.

The demons are assigned to you to cause you to continually fail. The demons are unleashed against you to prove the thoughts that they are telling you. For 29 years, I showed up an hour early to work, and I did not get paid for that. No matter what the devil threw at me, whether it was a bad storm or my car broke down and the devil was laughing, I was able to fulfill my commitments.

As a Christian, you are filled with the power of God, the Word of God, and the knowledge of God. If you still cannot imitate God, it is because you are in a war, and entities are contending for you. Even though those demons cannot get into your spirit to control you, they are going to use psychological warfare to get *you* to do something against the purposes of God. I wish someone had told me this a long time ago, but I was told a Christian could not have a demon. Christians are told, *"No weapon formed against you shall prosper"* (Isa. 54:17). Believers speak out all the Scriptures and do not feel any better. Jesus cannot be manipulated; Jesus is "I Am."

As a Christian, you are filled with the power of God, the Word of God, and the knowledge of God. If you still cannot imitate God, it is because you are in a war, and entities are contending for you.

If you tell Jesus, "I believed, and I was not healed," Jesus will point right at you and say, "My blood was enough; the stripes on My back were enough." He will put it right back at you. You were healed 2,000 years ago. In fact, you were healed before the foundation of the world because Jesus was slain from the foundation of the world (see Rev. 13:8). If you say, "I told a demon to leave, and it did not leave my house." Jesus will say, "My name is all-powerful; My name is enough. The demons have to leave." He will throw it right back at you.

When I met Jesus, He was not at all the way people had represented Him. Everything Jesus does is strategic, and every-thing He says is something that He has thought out. Jesus does not say anything unless He means it. When a Christian lies to you, or they steal from you, or they tell you they are going to be a certain place and they do not show up, that is demonic activity because God does what He says. God always thinks about what He is going to do, and then He does it, and that is His personality.

Too often, Christians get to the point where they are focused on things that are not eternally valuable, but they do not know it. It is part of the demonic attack to make them think that is their personality. They point out that the pictures on the wall are crooked and that nothing is nice. They notice that the church does not have carpet on the floor, and they cannot believe it. A thousand years from now, it is not going to matter, and you should not have come for the carpet. You came because you wanted to encounter the other realm, and you wanted to hear the Word of God.

You know how critical people can be. However, for us to win and be effective in this generation, we have to come into unity, walk in love, and consider others more than ourselves (see Phil. 2:3). It is not easy because everything competes for your attention. It is humbling when you hear how hungry people all over the world are, and how they will do anything for the Father.

You do not want to become like someone who will not minister unless there is a certain amount of money that comes in or a certain kind of water in their room or a special coffee. If you get to that place, you have lost your edge as a minister. You have people who want to hear the voice of God. The price for being a Christian is greater when the greater works come because the greater works have to do with greater influence where you start influencing nations. God starts to set it up.

When my friend got delivered of all those demons, it took him years to discover who he was because those demons had started to affect his personality. He is a very powerful

Christian minister today, but he said that he had gotten to the place where he did not know himself anymore. It took him a while to discover who he was because the demons had been such a part of his personality and his mind. Slowly, the person God intended him to be started coming forth.

> *Jesus said to him, "I am the way, the truth, and the life. No one comes to the Father except through Me."*
>
> —John 14:6

In every generation, God has leaders, and He causes them to be visited, and He tells them to do things that they cannot do. That is with all of us. God touches us with fire, and that fire starts to influence us and change us for a generation that needs the bar to be raised in us. We need to maintain that so that we can influence our environment instead of *it* influencing us.

These evil entities cannot manifest in a person's flesh unless they have been given permission to go in. If you look at all of Paul's writings, you can read how he was caught up in the Spirit, and he saw many more things than I saw. Paul stresses the fact that you cannot yield to the flesh, and he lists witchcraft as a work of the flesh. I am not afraid of witches, and they do not know what to do with me because every demon that they send to me comes back injured and worn out.

You think the reason that I have authority over demons is that I went to Heaven and came back? When you die and you go to Heaven, you are going to find out that when you were born again, your spirit went to Heaven (see Eph. 2:6). Your spirit belongs there, and in fact you are just visiting here. Peter said that we are aliens down here; we are foreigners and strangers in this world (see 1 Pet. 2:11). The world will never treat us the way that we deserve to be treated.

A demon cannot get into a Christian because they are sealed in the Holy Spirit, but they can try to change our thinking or change our personality so that we lose our edge. I am not talking to people who are going to hell. I am talking to people who are going to Heaven. However, out of that group, only a small number of people are affecting their environment instead of being affected by it.

A demon cannot get into a Christian because they are sealed in the Holy Spirit, but they can try to change our thinking or change our personality so that we lose our edge.

There is an influence that has to happen where the Holy Spirit takes over your personality and you become other-worldly. You become bold, you become sure of yourself, and when somebody asks you a question you answer with certainty. When there is a decision to be made, you make the decision. You have already determined in your heart what you are going to do and where you are going. The decisions that you make are based on your destination in Christ and not on the drama between point A and point B.

THE WAR OF IMAGES

When I was in Heaven, I saw that all the TV programming and every kind of media was created to program *you* into feeling drama in everything and creating it if it does not exist. You are being taught and educated on how to create drama out of nothing in your life. You become addicted to the release of the chemicals in your own body. You become addicted to your adrenaline and all the feel-good chemicals in your body. These highs even affect your thought processes.

When I was a little kid in elementary school, I used to dream about getting a million dollars. One time I bought fake money and filled my suitcase with it and brought it to school because I was a "businessman." I often had to go to my grandma's house just to get enough food to eat. I would pick apples for twenty-five cents a bushel and would bail hay for three dollars an hour in Pennsylvania. Poverty was not my friend, and I worked from the time I was 13 years old. I retired from Southwest Airlines when I was 55 years old. When I went to Heaven, Jesus said, "Because you have agreed to go back, you cannot fail. I am going to be with you, and I am going to make sure that you have everything you will ever need, and I will provide for you."

The feeling that you get when you open a suitcase and you see that million dollars—think about that for a couple of minutes. Picture it—a million dollars, and it is yours. That feeling is chemical because endorphins are being released in your body right now, and they follow through from your thought process. Whatever you imagine in your mind, your body sides with that and creates a feeling, an environment that you are actually part of. That is why Jesus said, *"Whoever looks at a woman to lust for her has already committed adultery with her"* (Matt. 5:28). Your body responds to your thoughts; it is not personally analyzing it. The war that we are in is about our imagination.

Whatever you image in your mind, your body sides with that and creates a feeling, an environment that you are actually part of.

God came off of His throne when the tower of Babel was being built (see Gen. 11:1-9). The Trinity agreed that if they did not go down and confuse the people, then whatever they *imagined* they would be able to do, and nothing would be withheld from them. They had to be stopped, and they were evil.

Chemicals in your body are released to follow through with your imagination. God did it that way because we were created in God's image. When God thinks of something, He speaks it out, and He frames worlds with it. That is why Jesus said, "Speak to this mountain; if you believe in your heart what you say with your mouth, it shall be done for you" (see Mark 11:23). Jesus framed the worlds with His words. The physical body is not personally analyzing everything you think. Your body is following through with the chemical release to give you the scenario of the reality of what you are thinking. That is why you have to be careful about how your personality is formed in your thinking processes. People do not understand that these demonic personalities can cause you to believe a certain way, but it is not scriptural.

A multimillionaire was told by God to leave Kathi and me 1.4 million dollars. When she passed, she left it to us. I saw that the same feeling that I had in elementary school when I opened that briefcase was the same feeling that came over me now. I am telling you this because the feeling from the chemicals in my body were exactly the same from elementary school when it happened in reality. The feelings that I had from childhood to now were the same, and there was no difference because I had already imagined it.

My wife and I decided to start giving money away, but we did not tell anyone. We did not buy a new car. We kept the same little old car whose top speed going downhill was 45 miles per hour. We did not buy any new clothes. We did not change a thing, and we still went to church, and we even tithed to other churches too. We secretly gave things away to people, helping the poor. We set up apartments for people escaping persecution from their countries and gave them furnishings and food. It was glorious, and I said to my wife, "Kathi, Jesus sent me back, and it is all rigged in my favor. I cannot lose." My perception of prosperity is different now.

Kathi and I walked into church one day, and there was a prophet there, and we sat down. The prophet stopped the sermon and asked us to stand, and he started prophesying about the million dollars that just came in and then talked about the next million that the Lord was sending us. That million took years to come in, but it came in also. I was not trying to do this. I could not; I was a flight attendant, and my wife was a hairdresser. What was happening had to do with the forming of thoughts, and it is very important to understand. God was changing our frame of mind concerning financial provision. He has plans to give you provision for your vision.

If you are in debt, are you in debt to God, or are you in debt to a world system? Well, you are *not* in debt to God because Jesus' blood has paid that price on the cross. Spiritually you have been forgiven, and you do not owe God anything except your whole life. You lay your life on the altar, and your life is not your own, but that is fine because you have been forgiven, and you are not going to hell. How about living down here? While you are waiting to go to Heaven, do you think that God wants you to hide in a bunker somewhere and wait for Him to come again? Or does God want you to rule and reign as kings in this life? Does He want you to bring in the harvest? I just shifted your thinking, and the chemicals in your body started to follow that train of thought.

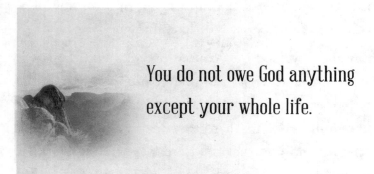

You do not owe God anything except your whole life.

I Am Just a Christian Who Prays in Tongues

When I retired from Southwest Airlines, they sent me all the paperwork to transfer my retirement out. The Lord gave me the name of a person whom I have never met, and I have not met him to this day, but he handles this type of thing. When I called him, he asked, "*How* did you hear of me?" I said, "Well, I am a Christian, and I pray in the Spirit, and your name came up. I looked you up, and I found that you are a financial advisor." He said, "Yes, I handle finances for many ministers." I said, "I am going to retire, and I need you to start the process for me."

I am telling you this for a reason because my mind falls behind God. It falls behind the curve because there is warfare. You need to be transformed by the renewing of your mind into what God is saying to you (see Rom. 12:2). I cannot be discouraged, because when I came back it was all rigged in my favor. If you are going to come to me and say, "Well, I believe this way," then I will ask you how that is working for you. I know what I believe and what is happening to me.

When the financial advisor transferred my retirement money out of Southwest Airlines, he called me. He said that I had six times more money than I should have had in there, and he needed me to tell him what happened. I told him that I was in Burbank, California, and I was feeding the poor one night. I would leave work, and instead of grabbing dinner, I would fast and buy food to hand out to homeless people. I wanted a double blessing so I would fast and hand those burgers out and witness to people on the streets.

One night I handed one to an angel that was undercover. The angel revealed himself and gave me the Word of the Lord. He told me that he was sent to tell me about the market crashes that were coming and told me what to do. I went home, and I told Kathi that there was a crash coming, and I had to get all my finances out into a money market fund. The money market would only provide half a percent return, but it was safe, so I did that. When the markets crashed in 2001, the fund that I had been in went down 80 percent. Then I waited until that fund changed direction, and I put the funds back in, and it went back up to normal again. I had almost doubled my money, and that happened in 2008.

Another angel came while we were in Seattle, Washington, and stood right beside me; Kathi was right there with me. The angel said that the market was going to crash again. I was looking at CNBC and the Dow was at the peak in July of 2008. I got on my laptop, and I slid everything out of my account again, and in September, there was another crash. In February of 2009, I put it all back in again, and this went on and on. All along, my thoughts and way of thinking were behind what God was doing. I retired, and I have six times as much in there that I should have, and I am not working anymore. There has to be something going on here because I am not *that* good. I know how to click with my mouse, but I do not know how to invest. I am not an investor, but I *am* a Christian who prays in tongues! I receive from Heaven because I pray in tongues constantly.

I am a Christian who prays in tongues! I receive from Heaven because I pray in tongues constantly.

Do you realize how your personality can be affected and cause you to lose out on what God wants to do? Moses was told by God to tell the people to borrow their neighbor's jewelry. That is stealing because they were not really going to borrow it, but they did it (see Exod. 12:35-36). Then the

Israelites convinced Pharaoh after ten plagues that they were going to go out and worship in the desert, but they borrowed the jewelry for life. God told Moses face to face to do this because God had a plan of deliverance. After they had been in captivity for over 400 years, their deliverance came to pass exactly as the prophet said it would.

When they came out of Egypt, they came out with the gold and the silver. In Psalms, it says that they came out with the abundance of Egypt. They had so much that when they went to build the Tabernacle in the desert, Moses had to stop the people from giving more because it was too much. When does that happen in the church? When did your pastor ever say not to give anymore because we have too much? I asked Jesus, "Was that stealing when the Israelites borrowed the jewelry, gold, and silver?" Jesus said, "No, it was not, because My people worked for free for 400 years, and I was just paying them back." I saw that they were just getting their lost wages back.

Do you see how your thinking shifts because everyone focuses on the controversies in the Bible? When you know the truth about it, you realize that God is righteous, just, and holy, and God favors His own people. You must allow the Holy Spirit to shift your thinking. If you do not allow the Holy Spirit to correct your thinking, you are going to meet Jesus, and you are going to find out that He is not Word of Faith and it is going to shock you. The Jesus I met is the ruler of everyone, the ruler of all men, and I cannot limit God by my thinking. When I met Jesus, His personality was so pure, and He did not limit me. The limitations were placed on me because I was in this fallen world, and I did not correctly discern the Lord's will based on His Word.

God is not a liar, and God cannot be mocked, and He is not going to say something and then not do it. The Lord told me to tell you that promotion comes from the Lord, and it is on the way. Promotion is on the way; it was designed before the foundation of the world that you would hear the Word of God, believe it, grasp it, and take it into you. God's Word produces a crop; it produces a harvest and a total transformation. You need to do the works of Jesus because the greater works are coming through the glory. God needs people who will step up and be who they are called to be and not be someone else.

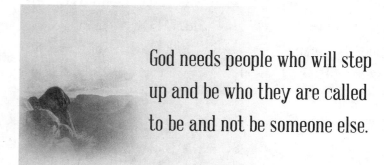

God needs people who will step up and be who they are called to be and not be someone else.

I do not know if you realize this, but I am not a musician, and yet I am on the Billboard charts. That should be hilarious and should show you that I am telling you the truth that God wants to do things in you and through you. God wants to show Himself to a generation with signs and wonders.

Chapter 5

RECEIVE YOUR BREAKTHROUGH

John answered and said, "A man can receive nothing
unless it has been given to him from heaven."
—JOHN 3:27

THE SOURCE OF EVERYTHING YOU RECEIVE COMES from Heaven. There is a transference from the heavenly realms. The transformation happens from the realm of the spirit where faith actually gets the title deed to what you have believed for and yanks it into this realm. You actually get the evidence before you get the actual object.

When you buy a house, you are at the title company and signing, and if you paid cash you get the title deed. You have that title deed, but you are still at the office with a lawyer completing the paper process. Once that transaction is complete, you have the house, but then you go through weeks of that person moving out and you moving in. There are all different processes that still have to happen; however, the transaction is done. Faith is the substance of things hoped for and the evidence of things not seen (see Heb. 11:1). Everything originates from Heaven, and I sense the reality of your breakthrough right now. I have the evidence inside of me of the breakthrough for you. There is a shockwave behind me because I broke through already, and the devil knows about it.

My friends fly fighter jets; they fly slightly faster than the speed of sound and produce a *boom* behind them, but they have already gone by before you encounter the sound. They've gone beyond the barrier of sound. The sound was following them as they passed on by. You can see the jet before you can hear it, and that is how it is with breakthrough. You see the breakthrough, but the barrier that you just broke through is behind you instead of in front of you.

In the Spirit, God can take you to your future. That is why we have dreams and visions. That is why the Word of the Lord comes to you and why you have words of knowledge and words of wisdom. God, by His Spirit, will come in and change your thinking for someone else as well as yourself, but it originates from Heaven. There is a transference that has to happen. You have to rely on the Spirit of God to help you to bring it into this realm.

The promotion is on its way right now. God sees everything, and He knows everything about you, and you need to receive the breakthrough in your spirit right now. As you start thinking about breakthrough, you can feel your body respond because there is a chemical that is released to get you ready for breakthrough. There is a good feeling that comes when you know you are going to break through.

The barrier that you just broke through is behind you instead of in front of you.

GREATER THAN JOHN

You yourselves bear me witness, that I said, "I am not the Christ," but, "I have been sent before Him." He who has the bride is the bridegroom; but the friend of the bridegroom, who stands and hears him, rejoices greatly because of the bridegroom's voice. Therefore this joy of mine is fulfilled. He must increase, but I must decrease.

—JOHN 3:28-30

John the Baptist would never have been on Christian TV. A conversation with a producer would have gone like this:

> PRODUCER: "Do you have a book that you can promote?"
>
> JOHN: "No."
>
> PRODUCER: "Well, do you have any sermons?"
>
> JOHN: "Just one, 'Repent for the Kingdom of God is at hand.'"
>
> PRODUCER: "Well, we need 28 minutes of programming. Do you have anything else?"
>
> JOHN: "No."
>
> PRODUCER: "How many miracles have you had in your ministry?"
>
> JOHN: "None."
>
> PRODUCER: "What do you do?"
>
> JOHN: "I baptize people, and I tell them to get right with God."
>
> PRODUCER: "We'll call you."

John would never have been on TV. He had no miracles, no six-second sermon, and no book, just came eating honey and locusts.

The breakthrough was happening, and John had to decrease so that Jesus could increase (see John 3:30). As soon as John said that he must decrease, Jesus had everyone look at John. Jesus said that there has never in history been anyone greater than John the Baptist in the kingdom (see Matt. 11:11).

However, Jesus went on to say, *"But he who is least in the kingdom of heaven is greater than he."* The least, the little toe in the body of Christ is greater than John the Baptist. There is hope for you, there was a shift, and a change is happening.

The least, the little toe in the body of Christ is greater than John the Baptist.

In Heaven, everything is based on cycles. On earth, we are in a timeline based on the Greek calendar with hash marks where there are reference points. That is not the way God is. God speaks, and where it begins is where it ends. When God breathed you into your mother's womb, the very spot where He breathed you in is where you will stand and give an account for your life because it is a cycle.

When Jesus brought me back and left me in the operating room, He turned to me, and He said something very special to me. Jesus smiled, and then He walked through this glorious door. I knew the exact age that I would be when I die, and I knew I would be right behind Him through that door, and it would only be about a minute and a half. I have lived twenty-six more years, and I have a whole bunch more. I know that when I go to Heaven that I will be behind Him through that door, and He will turn around and smile again at me. Jesus will say, "You decided to come," because, in Heaven, no time will have even elapsed. It is so rigged in our favor.

You are wondering how God can do all of this. How can God visit all these people and talk to them and help so many people in the world? How can Jesus visit you and visit me, Kevin, at the same time? In Heaven, if you started walking across the throne room, it would take you one day because that is how big it is. In earth time, it took God seven days to make the earth, six days in a row, and on the seventh day, He rested (see Gen. 1 and 2). God did not need the rest; He did that for us. It was not even lunchtime on the first day in Heaven, and God was just getting started. In Heaven, I saw Jesus talking to someone here, and then He was over there talking to someone, and then He was behind me, but I do not know how He got there. God messes with everything that you have made a boundary in your thought life.

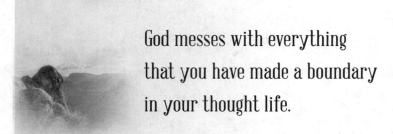

God messes with everything that you have made a boundary in your thought life.

When I died, Jesus showed me twelve people whom I was sent back for if I were to make the choice to return. It took me 22 years to meet all those people, and I knew their names and everything about them. I met them on my airplane, in a store, and in different states. I would call them by name, and they would say, "I have not told you my name yet." When I witnessed to them, every single one of them got saved. Jesus sent me back for people who were not even saved.

I have been to other countries that I had dreams about months before I ever went. I would find myself there in a dream, I knew the street names, and I knew what was going to happen next. I was in Germany with Kathi, and I knew every street around us even though I had never been to Germany before. I had already experienced it in the Spirit in a dream. I had a dream about South Africa, and I told Kathi that we were going to South Africa. It took six months before I was invited to go. The same thing happened with Australia, but it took almost two years before they finally called me.

Breakthrough comes from Heaven, and it is initiated by Heaven. It comes into this realm through you and your relationship with God through faith because God is framing your world. It has nothing to do with what you think; it is what you know based on the Word of God.

> *He who comes from above is above all; he who is*
> *of the earth is earthly and speaks of the earth. He*
> *who comes from heaven is above all. And what He*

has seen and heard, that He testifies; and no one receives His testimony.

—JOHN 3:31-32

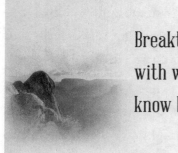

Breakthrough has nothing to do with what you think; it is what you know based on the Word of God.

This Scripture speaks of our Lord Jesus Christ from His realm. This is the real Jesus as He is in Scripture—a supernatural man who is God. Jesus is a God-Man who still has His body, and He is seated on His throne in Heaven. Jesus has identified with your weaknesses, and He beat the living daylights out of the devil for you and gave you the keys. Jesus said He would see you later, and while you are waiting, He has sent you a Helper (see John 14). Jesus said that the Helper, the Holy Spirit, would be like Him, and that Holy Spirit was going to enforce the blessing.

Did you know that the Holy Spirit is an Enforcer of the covenant and the blessing? The Holy Spirit inside of you is literally a Lawyer, Advocate, and Helper who says, "No, we are not doing it this way because it is written." The Holy Spirit is constantly bringing correction to anything that comes into your environment that is wrong. The Holy Spirit is historical because He changes history, and we are to write history with our lives.

One time the Lord handed me a blank check, and He said, "Name your price, I cannot resist you; I am buying you out. I want all of you." That will change your life. Then He handed me a blank sheet of paper and told me to write out His will for my life. I started praying in the Spirit, then I interpreted it, and then wrote down what the Holy Spirit had prophesied through me. Every time I have ever done that, it has all come to pass because I am connected to the vine, and I am a branch (see John 15).

You cannot pray bad prayers when the Holy Spirit, who is the Advocate Lawyer, is there to help you pray. The Holy Spirit will say, "No, you are going to go in, and you are going to say this. Do not say that, and do not answer that." That is what lawyers do; they want to answer for you. When I wrote out the will of God and it came to pass, I asked the Lord, "Why did You want me to do that?" Jesus said, "You have matured to the place where I trust you." The Lord trusts people.

The Lord trusts you; He gave you everything, and He invested in you. Now you are to produce fruit in keeping with repentance (see Matt. 3:8). You have to turn your face away from the world, and you must look at Jesus and stay focused on Him. If you turn away and you feel like something has caught your attention, you need to repent and turn your face back to His face. The Spirit of God is coaching you and telling you what you need to do.

The Lord trusts you; He gave you everything, and He invested in you. Now you are to produce fruit in keeping with repentance.

The Lord gave me the book *It's Rigged in Your Favor*, and in that book I challenge people by asking, "What would you do tomorrow if you knew you could not fail?" What that does is it judges you on the decisions you make every day based on the fear of failure instead of realizing that your breakthrough comes from Heaven. John the Baptist's ministry came from Heaven, and when it was time for him to back out and decrease, he did it. He took his six-second sermon, and he went and gave Herod a hard time and lost his head. John allowed Jesus to come forward.

THE SPIRIT OF PROPHECY

Jesus came forward after John, and it was Heaven's perfect timing. When Jesus ministered for three and a half years, Jesus had done enough for them to kill Him. Then the twelve disciples went out, and they did so much that they were also killed. Then the believers went out. Even the church in Jerusalem multiplied by the thousands in a matter of weeks because the fire that touched them from the other realm started spreading. No matter what happened, the Kingdom of God continued to increase, and the gates of hell could not prevail against the church.

The good news of the Gospel then went to other countries and other people adhered to it. Then believers got on a ship called the Mayflower, where over 30 people made a covenant with God. You should read the Mayflower Compact. They wrote a contract that gave this land of America to God, and God still honors that covenant today. A whole nation was influenced, and you can trace it back to obedient people like Elijah, Enoch, Moses, John the Baptist, Jesus, the disciples, and early believers. They would get flogged, stoned, thrown in jail, and they would be released and would go right back and pray for boldness to do it again. They would go right back to the center of the square and start testifying about Jesus again. A key is to testify about Jesus because it is the spirit of prophecy.

> *And I fell at his feet to worship him. But he said to me, "See that you do not do that! I am your fellow servant, and of your brethren who have the testimony of Jesus. Worship God! For the testimony of Jesus is the spirit of prophecy."*
>
> —REVELATION 19:10

When you yield to the spirit of prophecy, you take the breakthrough from the other realm and you implement it into your house, your family, your job, and into your church. Then when you pray, you have a command about you, and you are not just praying to pray. You want to receive from Heaven, and you tell the Lord that you do not care if you have to stay in your room for two days.

I have prayed like that with a prayer partner, and we would get to the place where we would pray like bulldogs. We were going to bite down, and we were not going to be denied. There has to be that part of you that comes forth out of your personality because satan does not want aggressive Christians. You must determine within yourself that you are going into your prayer closet and say, "I am not coming out until I receive from Heaven."

I am sure you have heard of Charles Finney and Brother Nash. Brother Nash would go on the train to a city that God would target, and he would check in to a room in a boarding-house. Then he would start praying, and every day he would peek out his window to see if people were falling when they walked by his window. Charles Finney would telegraph and ask if it was time to come yet, but Brother Nash would say, "Not yet," and would keep praying.

Brother Nash would look at the local bar, and if people were still going into the bar, he would keep praying. He prayed until he heard what sounded like a sack of potatoes fall in front of his door. When he looked and saw that a person had fallen and that nobody was going to the bar any longer, he would telegraph Finney. Nash would tell Finney that it happened and that it was time to come, and when Finney came, they would have revival. Brother Nash would go from city to city interceding ahead of Finney. When Brother Nash died, the revivals stopped.

Charles Finney was a lawyer who completed law school and was starting his private practice. One day while praying out in the woods pacing between two trees, the Lord told Charles to quit his law practice to become a minister. He gave up everything, and he accidentally yielded to the Spirit. He said to the Lord, "You don't think we are *not* going to have revival, do you?" The price had become very high, and Charles was going forward, but now a breakthrough from Heaven had to come. Just like it is coming for you right now. The heavenly realm came through Charles because he placed a demand on what he already knew was God's will, and you too can be bold about it.

I am not telling God to do something, but He is telling me this is what He wants to do, and when are we going to do it? I have found that the personality of Jesus Christ is "We are ready." If you knew how many times I have had angels come and say to me, "We are on the ground, and we are ready, do not wait," you would understand me better. These beings that are all around us have been sent to minister for us.

God's angels do not know defeat and do not think we are going to lose anything. They know God's plan, and they are trying to squeeze their world through you and are trying to push everything into manifestation. Angels are coming to work and ease the way all around you so that you can, even accidentally, yield to the Spirit of God. Angels are waiting for you to do a God action or give a God Word. It is so that the glory of God can be revealed, because Jesus came to destroy the works of the devil.

Angels are waiting for you to do a God action or give a God Word.

Life begins at the throne room of God, and the spirits of all created people do not just disappear because they came from God's breath. God cannot destroy a spirit. God cannot make a person's spirit go away because it is part of Himself, and it is part of His creation. God cannot make angels simply disappear, either. He can chain them up, and He can throw them into the lake of fire, but demons and spirits will always exist because when God creates something, it comes from Himself. We have the devil problem because angels left their abode, they left their boundaries, and then they were chained, but they do not cease to exist (see Jude 1:6). A human spirit does not cease to exist. Human spirits will live forever, with some of them bound by chains in hell, and some of them living in Heaven where everyone belongs.

> *And the angels who did not keep their proper domain, but left their own abode, He has reserved in everlasting chains under darkness for the judgment of the great day. ·*
>
> —JUDE 1:6

BREAKTHROUGH PRAYERS

Everything that God made in the beginning was good. God has these ideas about restoration and provision, using words like *breakthrough* and *impartation*. In a perfect world, we would not have to be taught things about prosperity, health, guidance, or hearing God's voice. We would not need to know any of these things, and you would not have to be reading this if you were still living in Eden. In Eden, God would show up and talk, and it would be at a different level because we would not be in need in the Garden of Eden, as we are now.

God has to introduce His heavenly realm, where His perfect will is, into our earthly life. When this happens, the result is that we experience breakthrough. Jesus instructed us to pray like this, "Our Father who art in Heaven, Holy be Your name. Thy kingdom come, Your will be done on the earth as it is in Heaven" (see Matt. 6:9-13). That is how we are supposed to pray, but if you start praying like that, you are going to get a lot of persecution. People are going to say that you are extreme because you are pulling what is in Heaven to the earth, but that is what Jesus said to do—to pray that what is in Heaven comes to earth.

Our heavenly Father has now given us the idea of breakthrough because of this fallen world. As a result of that fall, we now need breakthrough, impartation, and overthrow. We need weapons in order to win in the warfare. God has to implement strategies into our lives that push the darkness out. We must have extreme amounts of light from Heaven coming into our life through knowledge and understanding. We need the Word of God preached to us many times over, and not just once. We need to hear it and hear it until the seed in our hearts starts to grow, and that seed produces a crop. When the seed produces a crop, you have a harvest, and that harvest is the souls of men. Everything that we do should be with this in mind, that we are turning outward and helping people. We are sharing the truth in order for them to be set free. That is what being a follower of Jesus Christ is all about; being about our Father's business.

We must have extreme amounts of light from Heaven coming into our life.

You are not supposed to be waiting for the antichrist to come forth and trying to calculate his name and number, figuring out when you are going to have to build your bomb shelter and know if the store is going to have the water that you like for your stockpile. Christians watch this stuff too much, and it starts to change you to where you do not need breakthrough anymore; you need a bunker and some beans. My military friends who are special forces tell me that under martial law, those who are storing up will have their property become special forces headquarters. They will thank you for setting it up for them.

Everything is being delayed so that the harvest can come in. Jesus explained to me that there are people who concentrate a lot on prophecy and end-time things. People who do that will get to a place where they are self-sufficient, and then they do not leave room for angels to come and bring food or to protect them. I want the supernatural, and I want to have provision from Heaven.

There has to be a turn, and that turn comes when we begin to have an understanding of words like *breakthrough, impartation, transformation,* and *translation* because these words are revolutionary. Have you ever noticed that there are certain men and women of God who show up and the whole atmosphere changes? You can enjoy their world for a weekend, but when you go home you cannot take it with you. The Holy Spirit who came into you wants to minister through you, but He wants to talk about Jesus. The Holy Spirit wants to take Jesus and feed Him to the people, and He also wants to meet your needs. The Holy Spirit's ministry is talking about what the Father wants to say so you cannot talk about yourself.

We need ministers, and all of us are ministers, on one level or another, as servants of God. We dish out what is from Heaven and give it to the people because if we only give them a psychological fix or if we only give them money, we have not resolved the deeper spiritual problem. Jesus wants disciples; He wants permanent family. My wife Kathi and I have committed our ministry to the Lord, and I said, "Lord, we will do this ministry if You will promise that it will be permanent everywhere we go." When we teach, people will continue to sense the atmosphere from Heaven and walk in it, so it is a permanent change in their lives.

The idea of breakthrough, the idea of your mind changing, has to do with the realities that are in Heaven being yanked into this realm. Jesus did it all the time. Jesus would speak the truth, but the Pharisees, the religious people, would come at Him and confront Him. The Pharisees attacked Jesus because they were jealous and because they could not produce what He was producing.

Breakthrough happens when Jesus smiles at you when He speaks something, and it is supposed to be permanent. It is supposed to influence you forever, not make you feel good for a mere moment and then you forget what He said. What changes you is the impartation of the Word, the intent of God's Word. It goes into you, and it produces a crop. The born-again experience is not something you can explain, but you know that there was a definite change in you. Something happened to me because everything old had passed away, and all things became new (see 2 Cor. 5:17). I still had warfare, and I had to manage my flesh, and I had to manage my mind.

What changes you is the impartation of the Word, the intent of God's Word. It goes into you, and it produces a crop.

Christians who do not discipline their flesh and do not transform their minds by the Word of God can experience chaos in their lives. These people say, "I don't know how this happened." I can tell you what happened; it happened one step at a time. You cannot blame God for things that have happened. Why did that person die of cancer? You do not know the circumstances. Perhaps that person was being told for years not to eat certain things. You cannot do that anymore.

If I had not gone to Heaven and encountered Jesus, I would not be able to tell you this, but you are never going to stand before Jesus and blame Him for anything. You are never going to do it because He has provided everything we need for life and godliness down here, and part of that is the healing power of God. Part of that provision is guidance, and a part is deliverance. If you have a devil problem, the devil has to go. I do not care if the devil spits at me or if he laughs at me because that devil is going. The devil is a liar, and anything he says is a lie. He has not impressed me a bit.

RECEIVING HIS WORD IN THE SPIRIT

But he who is joined to the Lord is one spirit with Him.
—1 CORINTHIANS 6:17

Breakthrough occurs when God introduces the other realm, so when you pray you must pray from Heaven to the earth. How do you do that? The part of you that is from Heaven is your spirit. Paul told the Corinthians, "When you join yourself to the Lord, you are one with Him in spirit." If that is the case, then if the Lord is talking, you are listening. Think about that, and if He is inside of your spirit, then you are Spirit to spirit. If the Lord says something to you, then where He is saying it is the same place you hear it.

I do not talk about Jesus as though He is sitting on a throne because He is right here, right now. Jesus promised me that if I came back, He would come and talk to me, and I am to tell the people what He says, and then they will be rerouted for the rest of their lives. God is a Spirit, and He speaks to you in your spirit, and He communicates with you Spirit to spirit. God is a Spirit, so everything He does is from that realm. In the New Covenant, the Spirit of God is inside of you, and the same place that He talks to you is the same place that you hear Him, and there is no space. If you cannot hear God's voice, then what is the reason? The discrepancy is if you have not built yourself up in the areas of God's language, then you do not understand the ways of God.

Breakthrough is here, it is imminent, but we are waiting for some sort of manifestation or something supernatural to happen. What if it is a lifestyle? You want to be around consistent people, and you do not want people to be exclusionary, where everything they talk about is how holy they are and that they are such a man of God. I do not need someone to read the Bible for me, and I do not need to go to a person to confess my sins. I have *the* High Priest. I can go into the Holy of Holies myself with Him. You have to be careful because ministry is not to be exclusionary. Ministry is not where only certain people encounter God, because that is what has happened in every generation. When that happens, a lot of people get eliminated because they stop seeking God, and they are letting others do it for them.

All of us are supposed to be building each other up in the unity of the faith. Everyone is supposed to be encountering the supernatural. I do not draw these lines in ministry. I do not exclude people from seeking and knowing God, and I tell people all my secrets. I tell them what they must do to know Him, and I tell them how the Spirit realm works, and I want to give it away freely. Ministry is about the Spirit of God bringing Heaven to earth, and it is about introducing the supernatural into your world. Ministry is something that the Holy Spirit does for you every day. You do not need me to come to your house; you need God to come to your house. I want to light a fire and throw an extra gallon of gas on and start a fire that even the devil cannot put out. I want to take a coal from the altar and place it in a person by impartation.

Ministry is about the Spirit of God bringing Heaven to earth, and it is about introducing the supernatural into your world. You do not need me to come to your house; you need God to come to your house.

For the word of God is living and powerful, and sharper than any two-edged sword, piercing even to the division of soul and spirit, and of joints and marrow, and is a discerner of the thoughts and intents of the heart.

—HEBREWS 4:12

The sword that is being described here is the sword of the Spirit; it is the Word of God. Jesus is the Word, and He is a Person, and the Holy Spirit is also a Person as well. They are individuals who come from another realm called the spirit realm. They have come to live with you, and they have announced breakthrough in your life.

THE GIFTS OF THE SPIRIT

The spiritual gifts are given to build up the body of Christ. The transaction happens when we yield and allow the Holy Spirit to manifest through the gifts of the Spirit. Whatever gifts God has given, you can start to work in your life as you yield. Yielding fulfills the law and fulfills the purpose and intents of the church of Jesus Christ. Using your gifts allows the Spirit of Truth to push out darkness, evil, and lies. It allows the law of the Spirit of Life in Christ Jesus to break the power of the law of sin and death (see Rom. 8:2). There are physical laws, and there are spiritual laws. Once we come to the unity of the faith, then we can participate in the ministry of the body of Christ outwardly to the world. God loves us all and ministers to the saved and the unsaved.

> *But one and the same Spirit works all these things,*
> *distributing to each one individually as He wills.*
>
> —1 CORINTHIANS 12:11

God gives us gifts individually as the Spirit wills. Paul said that there are impartations from Heaven called *gifts* and that there are certain ministry governments of God, which are called the five-fold ministry of the church. God sets in the church some to be apostles, prophets, pastors, teachers, and evangelists. God sets these in the church to bring us to the unity of the faith.

> *And He Himself gave some to be apostles, some*
> *prophets, some evangelists, and some pastors and*
> *teachers, for the equipping of the saints for the work*
> *of ministry, for the edifying of the body of Christ,*
> *till we all come to the unity of the faith and of the*
> *knowledge of the Son of God, to a perfect man, to*
> *the measure of the stature of the fullness of Christ.*
>
> —EPHESIANS 4:11-13

You cannot wake up in the morning and say you are called to one of these five-fold offices and then go and print yourself a certificate off the internet; God Himself does the calling. When you are called of God to one of the five-fold offices of the church, you are held accountable, and you walk with God humbly. The Holy Spirit helps you to develop into the area that you are called. All of the prophets I know do not want to be prophets because the price is so great. Most people who are called to these five-fold ministries know the price that they must pay to be in that. It diminishes the office when people claim to be something that they are not, and they do not pay the price.

> *But the manifestation of the Spirit is given to each one for the profit of all: for to one is given the word of wisdom through the Spirit, to another the word of knowledge through the same Spirit, to another faith by the same Spirit, to another gifts of healings by the same Spirit, to another the working of miracles, to another prophecy, to another discerning of spirits, to another different kinds of tongues, to another the interpretation of tongues.*
> —1 CORINTHIANS 12:7-10

There are nine gifts of the Spirit, also known as impartations of the Spirit, that God can put into us as He wills. These gifts drive out darkness, set people free, and they can minister through you to other people. The Spirit will speak to you concerning a situation, and you have to speak it out, you have to yield to the Spirit and let that come forth because it is going to change and help someone else. You have to yield to the Spirit. In your own house, the Spirit of God might want you to say something, and no one is around, but if you had your spiritual eyes opened, you would see there are plenty of little invisible entities around.

The Word of God is powerful and active, and the gifts of the Spirit are powerful and active, and they come from the other realm. The Word of God did not originate from man; the men of old were moved by the Holy Ghost and wrote (see 2 Pet. 1:21). That is how the Word of God came to pass; it did not originate from men, but it originated from Heaven. The Gospels are a journal of things that Jesus did and said on earth, but if you get into the meat of the matter, you must read what Paul and Peter wrote. I am talking about the inside information of the Spirit realm from behind the scenes. They wrote about what Jesus bought for you. What Jesus did behind the scenes in the Spirit realm is in Paul's writings, and he explains everything that was going on. You would understand by the Gospels alone what you received positionally with Jesus Christ. However, it is the give-and-take of the disciple's questions that helps us to understand doctrinally what Christ has done for us.

Your walk with God has manifestations of the gifts of the Spirit, and they are given individually as the Spirit wills for the building up of the saints. Everyone needs a word, but they need a word of confirmation. They do not need guidance from you, but they do need confirmation of what God is speaking to them. If you are a prophet, then you are going to speak from the truth in the Spirit of God. What you are going to speak to someone is going to be confirmation of what God is saying to the person, and it is not going to be something new. "Those who are led by the Spirit of God are sons of God," according to Romans chapter eight. It does not say that those who are led by prophets of God are sons of God. You must be led by the *Spirit* of God.

YOU *CAN* HEAR FROM GOD

But you are a chosen generation, a royal priest-hood, a holy nation, His own special people, that you may proclaim the praises of Him who called you out of darkness into His marvelous light.

—1 PETER 2:9

The New Covenant has placed us in a situation where we are all priests and kings of the Most High God (see also Rev. 1:6). We are all prophetic in the sense that all of us can hear from God, and we can speak on behalf of God. I am not diminishing the office of prophet, but I am actually putting it up on a pedestal by saying that there are very few legitimate prophets. A word from God can shift a whole family's life and possibly a whole generation if that man or woman does what the confirmed word is telling them.

How is it then, brethren? Whenever you come together, each of you has a psalm, has a teaching, has a tongue, has a revelation, has an interpreta-tion. Let all things be done for edification.

—1 CORINTHIANS 14:26

Every one of us has gifts of the Spirit inside of us, so you need to pray and let the Holy Spirit show you. In a Spirit-filled atmosphere, you will feel those gifts start to activate. The atmosphere was so powerful in Corinth that Paul provided advice on bringing order to the church. He explained to them that he knew everyone had a word, a tongue, or a song, but that everything must be done in order. He advised them to choose a few at a time and have them line up, but not to interrupt the speaker. He let them know that the Holy Spirit speaks through the leader, so the church is to yield to leadership. He advised that they should speak as the Spirit wills and that if your gift was that of tongues, then you were to make sure that someone could interpret (see 1 Cor. 14:27-33).

A word from God can shift a whole family's life and possibly a whole generation if that man or woman does what the confirmed word is telling them.

In the corporate setting at that time, the environment of Heaven was so strong in those meetings that Paul had to give directions to keep it orderly. Today you might get one person who is brave enough to come up and give a message in tongues, an interpretation, or a word of knowledge. In most meetings, nobody does it, but it should not be that way. Everyone should have a psalm, a teaching, a tongue, a word, or an interpretation.

But if the Spirit of Him who raised Jesus from the dead dwells in you, He who raised Christ from the dead will also give life to your mortal bodies through His Spirit who dwells in you.

—ROMANS 8:11

When you use the gift that the Holy Spirit gave you, there is a shift that happens in the atmosphere. The power that raised Jesus from the dead is within you, and that same power is going to quicken your mortal body. I encounter the supernatural every day because I have chosen to put myself in a place where it happens; it happens when you let Heaven invade your life. It is not just about being a Christian. Jesus was revolutionary, and He did not keep quiet; He spoke, He confronted, He drove out demons, He healed the sick, and He raised the dead. It is part of what Christianity is, and we are not supposed to be victims.

The power that raised Jesus from the dead is within you, and that same power is going to quicken your mortal body.

Now I know that it says to turn the other cheek, and I get that (see Matt. 5:39). I asked Jesus about being innocent as a dove and as shrewd as a serpent, and I told Him that I wanted to know what it meant (see Matt. 10:16). Jesus told me that when you approach a snake, he always rears up to protect himself, but he does not strike. A snake is very shrewd and does not trust anyone because he's cursed, and he is on the ground, and it is not easy for him to get away. He has learned to rear up and get ready to protect himself, and Jesus told me to be like that but be as innocent as a dove. You are not here to be a victim because Jesus has already beat the devil's brains out, and He wants you to do the same. He wants you to enforce what He already did.

> *But this Man, after He had offered one sacrifice*
> *for sins forever, sat down at the right hand of God,*
> *from that time waiting till His enemies are made*
> *His footstool.*
> —HEBREWS 10:12-13

The author of the Book of Hebrews is talking about Jesus here. You can get to where God abides with you in the heavenly place, and you start to function there permanently. You will not need to go from meeting to meeting to get your fix because you will be going to meetings to minister and getting to know people to love them and build them up. You will go and gather together, and you will come and play your musical instruments. You will have a word, an encouragement, and you will want to pray for people.

You begin to walk in this place where you are part of what God is doing, and it is revolutionary. Everywhere that Jesus went, He offended the Pharisees because that religious system could not reproduce what Jesus was doing. They did not have the authority and the power that Jesus had, and the people knew it. The Pharisees were losing the people, and that is what happens even today when churches do not produce.

What happens when people in ministry do not obey God? What happens is that God keeps moving, and they do not. The result of someone not obeying God affects everyone around them, especially if you are in leadership or ministry. If someone does not give the word of God one weekend, then you are going to feel the void; you can feel something is missing. You did not get your package, and it was because someone did not deliver it. If someone does not deliver or impart what is coming out of them by the Holy Spirit, then you get robbed. This loss can happen every Sunday and sometimes every Wednesday and Friday night too. No one discerns how important they are and the price that needs to be paid.

One time, when I was in pain, I had called off sick from my job at the airlines, which at the time I hardly ever did. Even when I was sick, I never liked to call off because I wanted to be a good employee. It is hard to fly for 13 hours a day feeling sick, but I did it for years, and I finally just thought I would call off. I was lying there in pain with my wife, and we were reading our Bibles when an angel of the Lord walked into the room as clear as day. He did not have wings, did not say a word, he had no armor on, but he was a bright shining minister of fire who was smiling and very happy. The angel did not speak as he walked over to my side of the bed and placed two fingers on me, and suddenly every symptom left. I could not feel the bed anymore because I was floating, and I was completely healed. Just before he walked out of the bedroom door, the angel turned and smiled at me and said, "That is how easy it is to be healed."

This experience messed with my doctrine because I thought you have to lay hands on the sick for them to recover. Where is the oil, and where are the elders? Can angels heal people? Yet here it was happening to me. Those who are in the body of Christ are the ones who are supposed to be carrying this. We should not be showcasing the five-fold ministry of the church. I got healed, and I realized that the other realm has healing in it, and this realm does not. Doctors can only assist the body in healing itself, but we need a touch from the other side.

Peter was probably the least of the candidates to be an apostle, but when he got it right, he would walk down the street, and his shadow would touch people, and they would be healed. He did not have a camera on them to sensationalize it and then take an offering. Peter just walked down the street, and he was not even trying to believe. Maybe we are supposed to get back to a lifestyle of walking. The next time you are at restaurant, what if you have a vision of the person who is waiting on you and the power of God is so strong, and you say, "Thus says the Lord." You start to prophesy to that young lady, telling her how the Lord has a plan for her life, and not to be so fast in marrying her boyfriend. I have been in restaurants where this has happened, just like you are going to do because you yield to the Holy Spirit.

You might not think that you are significant, but you can see that it is more about *you* than you would like to admit. It is about you allowing God to place you in a position where you have the say-so in a situation. God needs one brave person to agree with Him and start to shift the atmosphere and shift a whole generation. You can shift a whole generation, and the walls of China could come down through intercession, and you do not even have to visit the wall.

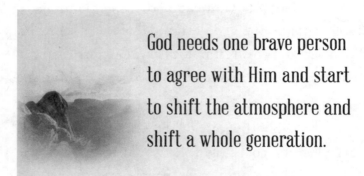

God needs one brave person to agree with Him and start to shift the atmosphere and shift a whole generation.

An angel of the Lord came to Paul in the night, and the angel said, "Do not be afraid, Paul; you must be brought before Caesar" (see Acts 27:24). No matter what would happen to Paul, whether he was bitten by a snake, shipwrecked, or beaten, the angel would appear to him. Paul went through so much, and it makes you *wonder*—why you are going through so much stuff? What is happening is that you are destroying the works of the devil everywhere you go.

There is a point where the devil is waiting for what you are going to do next to *him* instead of you waiting for what he is going to do to *you*. Everything you go through is setting you up for God to reward you. Even when the devil is working against you, the Lord comes in and repays you. What you have gone through literally provokes the heavenly realm, and God gets off His throne and comes because God is provoked. If satan is mocking God by hurting you, He will get up off His throne because He is a Warrior (see Zeph. 3:17).

SEATED WITH CHRIST

But God, who is rich in mercy, because of His great love with which He loved us, even when we were dead in trespasses, made us alive together with Christ (by grace you have been saved), and raised us up together, and made us sit together in the heavenly places in Christ Jesus.
—EPHESIANS 2:4-6

This thought that God has raised us up to sit together in heavenly places is foreign to a lot of Christians. I know, because I was one of them. However, I began to learn things as I expanded and found people who were preaching the actual Gospel. I started to realize that certain people had broken through the religious system, and the Spirit of God was able to speak revelation through them. I started to operate in that revelation that is in the body of Christ and the different ministry gifts. I have always learned something from everyone, even my enemies.

I have learned from witches who put curses on me and tried to trip me up. I study my enemy, and then I wait to find their weak points, and I take them out, and they never know what happened to them. These demons are real, and they go back and report. We are not wrestling against flesh and blood here but against principalities and powers (see Eph. 6:12). Paul said that these evil spirits have been brought to nothing by what Jesus had done (see Col. 2:15).

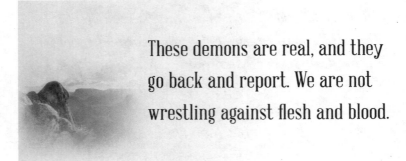

These demons are real, and they go back and report. We are not wrestling against flesh and blood.

It is important to study Jesus and what He did and then to study Paul and what he reiterates and comments on. Paul opens up the heavenlies to us in Ephesians, Colossians, and Philippians when he talks to us about what we have access to in Christ Jesus. He tells us what Jesus did for us behind the scenes, and you find out that Jesus was on a conquest, and He won. Implementing what Jesus has for us into this life is not as easy as I would like it to be; that is why I do what I do.

There is such a need at this point for everyone to operate in what they are called to do. *"The spirit indeed is willing, but the flesh is weak"* (Matt. 26:41). What you are going through is common, but very few people break through and find the narrow way. When I met Jesus face to face, I realized that I only had a portion of the revelation of who He is, but it is possible to know the personality of God. It is possible to know His ways. *"He made known His ways to Moses, His acts to the children of Israel"* (Ps. 103:7).

Moses knew God's ways because he went up on the mountain with God for 40 days at a time, but the people of Israel stayed down on the plain (see Exod. 19). They saw the manifestation of the mountain on fire, but they would not approach God because they did not know Him as a Father. Moses had a proper relationship with the Father, and he was a friend of God, but the people did not have that relationship, and they were afraid of God.

Moses walked right into that cloud in that fire, and he spent 40 days up there with God. Moses' face was transformed back to that of Adam, and it showed out the light of God. While Moses was looking at God, everything started to change. I was told that Moses went back to the replica of the origin of what the architect, God, designed man to be. Moses looked like Adam before the fall just by the association of being face to face with God, and he reverted to the original stock of how we should look. When Moses came back down from the mountain, the people were so afraid of his radiant face that he had to wear a veil (see Exod. 34:35).

God has instituted an acceleration in these last days, and we need to make disciples of all nations and not just converts. Jesus said, *"Go therefore and make disciples of all the nations"* (Matt. 28:19). That is different from a convert. We all need to be converted, but we also need to become disciples. I found myself seated with Christ in the heavenly realms, and there were myriads of angels and saints worshiping God at the throne. I knew it was at the end of the age, and the Lamb that was slain was seated beside me, and He was receiving the reward for His suffering, and I was not about to interrupt Him. Jesus was basking in these gold substances coming out from the saints as far off as I could see. Angels were falling and crying out, and they were singing this song, and they were all in tune; there was no soloist. It was everyone in one accord singing the *song of the redeemed*. It was beautiful, but it shook Heaven. Imagine millions and millions of angels and saints singing the *song of the redeemed* all in one accord, and Jesus was getting hit by the glory that was coming from everyone's mouth. The glory was hitting Jesus and washing over Him. Jesus was reclining on His throne and was receiving His reward for His suffering.

I tried to look at the Father's face, but just then Jesus sat forward and blocked me. I would not have been able to come back to my body if I had seen God's face. In man's fallen state, if you see the face of your Father in Heaven, you go right back to the original, and your earthly body cannot handle that and live. That was why God told Moses that he could not see God's face and live (see Exod. 33:20). God told Moses to hide in the cleft of the rock, and God passed by and let him look at His back. God knew Moses needed to live a little longer and finish his job on earth. After spending 40 days twice on the mountain with God, Moses could not die, and so God had to take him home when Moses was 120 years old and in perfect health.

Imagine millions and millions of angels and saints singing the *song of the redeemed* all in one accord, and Jesus was getting hit by the glory that was coming from everyone's mouth.

If you are going to spend time around God, you are going to live forever, and your body is going to be affected by that. You are going to be changed and transformed, and your body is going to receive resurrection power, which is going to quicken you. You are going to keep living until God says you are going to die. When I was there at the river of life, I knew if I took a drink of that water that I would live a thousand years. I knew that, and I was not allowed to drink it, but I wanted to. It looked like liquid diamonds, and I knew if I drank it, my body would not deteriorate anymore. There is no death in Heaven, and everything about God is successful, and there is no failure. In Heaven, there is no deterioration, no mishaps; there is nothing negative happening.

Everything about God is successful.

ANSWERS AT THE THRONE

God is not worried or upset if you ask for too much, and He is not going to dim the lights of Heaven if you start asking. The president of one of the schools that I graduated from had pastored for 11 years before he went and founded the school I attended. He had trained an intercessory group of women in his church, and they met every Monday. Jesus had appeared to this man eight times and had taught him how to pray, and he taught the intercessors how to pray.

The pastor would announce at the Sunday night service to make sure that everyone sent their prayer requests in before the end of the service because the women met on Monday to pray. He would tell his congregation that they better make sure that this is what they want because the intercessors would get it for them. Every single request that was written, people would get, so the pastor had to have that disclaimer. He had trained those intercessors to go after it, and they would not take no for an answer. There is a place in God where you can *"Ask what you desire, and it shall be done for you"* (John 15:7). You have to know God's ways.

> *If then you were raised with Christ, seek those things which are above, where Christ is, sitting at the right hand of God. Set your mind on things above, not on things on the earth.*
> —COLOSSIANS 3:1-2

When I was in the throne room, I knew of Ephesians 2:6, that we are made to sit in heavenly places with Jesus, but I did not understand the concept. I did not understand the concept of being a co-heir with Jesus Christ (see Rom. 8:17). Or the idea that we are fellow servants with Christ and that we are all children of God and Jesus is our brother and fellow heir with us. He is the Son of God, and we are sons and daughters of God. Jesus fixed me by taking me and sitting me on a throne beside Him in the heavenly realms, where I did not feel that I deserved to be. I wanted to get off that throne and get down there on the front row and fall on my face with those angels and start worshiping God. I felt uncomfortable because Jesus was being worshiped, and the Father was being worshiped, and I was seated there.

To him who overcomes I will grant to sit with Me on My throne, as I also overcame and sat down with My Father on His throne.
—REVELATION 3:21

While I was sitting there, I decided that I would go and sneak down because Jesus had His eyes closed. I was reaching down with my right foot to feel the floor. I thought if I could get my big toe down, I could find out where the floor was, and I could slip off. There was this place where you could go down and come around to the front, and so I was planning to do that. Jesus immediately sat up and looked at me, and He said, "Where are you going?" I said, "Well, I want to go down and worship You." Jesus said, "Oh no, I bought this for you; this is yours." It was years later that I found all these verses to support my experience. It took me a long time to find everything in the Bible that Jesus had told me. I was a scholar, and I had a degree, and I knew nothing.

What Jesus told me next changed my life forever. He said, "This is where you come in prayer." What He was saying was that you should pray from Heaven to the earth; you do not pray from earth to Heaven. Then He said this, "You come here in prayer, and you sit with Me until you get your answer, and then you take the answer back to the earth with you, and that is prayer." I had never heard this in my life. Jesus said, "There are no questions at the throne, only answers."

From then on, whenever I pray, I go to the throne, and I sit there with Jesus. I wait on Him, and then I let the will of God, the character of God, the personality of God start to come up within my spirit. The Holy Trinity is within proximity to every one of us. The Holy Spirit is within us and is wanting to bring up answers, not questions, and so I start to have answers before the questions are ever asked. I start to find myself in a place that I do not even know I am supposed to be at yet, but I find myself there in the perfect will of God.

When I pray like this, everything starts to come into sync, and I start feeling synchronized with Heaven and the angels. The angels love it because their work is really easy when you are not stiff-necked. When you do not resist the movement of the Spirit in your life, you can still go to work and function in this realm and function in the Spirit realm as well. It takes practice for you to master it, and it is not easy, but you can do it.

COVERED BY GOD

The Lord visited Cain because he did not offer a blood sacrifice; he offered the fruit of the earth, which was cursed (see Gen. 4). Cain was supposed to go to Abel, his brother, and get a lamb, but he did not do it. God had shown Cain and Abel's parents the proper way to sacrifice. When Adam and Eve sinned, they had taken fig leaves to cover themselves. God, however, required a blood sacrifice for sin, so He killed the animals and covered Adam and Eve with their skins. They then knew what a proper sacrifice to God was and what was required.

The Lord did not respect Cain's offering, and God visited Cain face to face. The Lord said to Cain, *"If you do well, will you not be accepted? And if you do not do well, sin lies at the door. And its desire is for you, but you should rule over it"* (Gen. 4:7). God Himself was coaching Cain, but what did he do? Cain took his brother out into the field and killed him, and Abel's blood had a voice, and it cried out to God. The Lord said to Cain, "Where is your brother? Your brother's blood cries out to Me." A blood sacrifice was required, and Cain did not do right because sin had mastered Cain and took him over. The wording there in Hebrew is, "sin is crouching as a lion at your temple door. Sin is like a crouching lion that desires to devour you, but you must master it."

I asked the Lord, "Why were You so mad that you cursed the fig tree?" He said, "As soon as Adam and Eve saw that they were naked, they grabbed the first thing that was close to them, and that was a fig leaf. That meant that they were right by a fig tree. Jesus said, "Covering themselves with a fig leaf was man's solution to the sin problem; Mine was blood. I was going to the cross in a couple of days, and when I saw that tree, I was reminded of why I came. I cursed the religious system that covers sin but does not take care of it. I cursed the religious system, and I cursed that tree."

Religion does not bear any fruit. Jesus was destroying man's way of taking care of sin.

That tree that Jesus cursed had no fruit on it because religion does not bear any fruit, so He cursed it. Jesus was destroying man's way of taking care of sin, and He cursed the tree at its roots. That is what Jesus does in our life. He curses our system of taking care of things, and He asks us to do the right thing, and that takes blood—the blood of Jesus. When you accept the blood of Jesus, you have done right, and sin cannot have you.

> *You stiff-necked and uncircumcised in heart and ears! You always resist the Holy Spirit; as your fathers did, so do you.*
> —ACTS 7:51

You do not want to resist God's ways, and whatever He says is the way that it is. There is nothing that you can do to better yourself in the flesh as far as your position with God. The blood of Jesus is what has eradicated sin, and it has taken care of the sin problem. That means that if you have repented of your sins, then your past does not exist. God can never hold your sins against you because He is just. If Jesus fulfilled the need for forgiveness through His blood, that means that it is done forever. You cannot feel guilty about your past if you have repented of your sins. You can never visit that sin again because your case is closed.

> *There is therefore now no condemnation to those who are in Christ Jesus, who do not walk according to the flesh, but according to the Spirit.*
>
> —ROMANS 8:1

In Heaven, Jesus showed me that the files with all my sins in them had been destroyed, and He did not know my past. Jesus was not allowed to know because His blood had taken it completely away. Jesus talked to me for that 45 minutes as though I had never sinned. It bothered me because I knew that He did not know, and Jesus treated me as though I was perfect. He talked to me about the coming age, and I was looking in Jesus' eyes, and I could tell that He did not know my past. He does not know your past.

So many Christians wrap themselves up in prophecy and all the things about the red dragon and the antichrist. You get to the point where you are just surviving and waiting. If you read Thessalonians, Paul was addressing this very thing. The believers had quit their jobs because they thought Jesus was coming back then. That was why Paul told them that if they did not work, then they could not eat (see 2 Thess. 3:10). The Thessalonians literally thought Jesus was coming back any moment, and as you know, theoretically, He is.

Jesus said to me, "I do not know when I am coming back as I am not allowed to know." I believe He would tell everyone if He knew ahead of time. The Father is the only one who knows. Not even the angels know, and neither does the Holy Spirit. Jesus did tell me that a sign would be when China's walls fall, and a whole lot of Chinese people come into the Kingdom, and then the Middle East falls to the Lord, and then Russia comes into the Kingdom. He told me that there would be a huge harvest that comes in, and that was the Father's heart. Until that time, we are working in the fields. Working for the Lord at your job and everywhere you go even when you go shopping, you are working to bring in the harvest. Jesus said this to me, and the way He said it made me realize that I am not down here surviving. I am down here qualifying for my next position in the next dispensation, and you have to accept this.

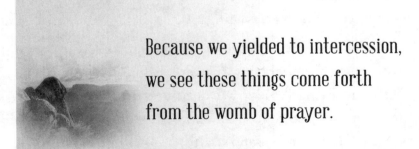

Because we yielded to intercession, we see these things come forth from the womb of prayer.

You have to resolve this in your mind, that this is the personality of God. God thinks generationally. When we intercede, we are birthing for the next generation, and we are answers to the previous generation's prayers. We will see the fruit of our prayers in the next generation, even though we might be in Heaven. Because we yielded to intercession, we see these things come forth from the womb of prayer.

You know we are at the end because every time a deliverer was in the womb of a woman, satan perpetrated mass murder. When Moses was in the womb, the demon that was in Pharaoh caught wind of it and had all the babies executed to try to get Moses. When Jesus came in the womb, Herod caught wind of it and had every baby executed before a certain age. Now in this generation, abortion was legalized in 1973. That means that satan has caught wind that the prophetic voice of the last generation is in the womb. There is a mass murder going on because the mass murderer is on the earth, and he has caught wind that the prophets are going to be born in the womb. The voices of John the Baptist that have the message and preach the coming of the Lord in the Spirit and power of Elijah are coming forth.

There are more babies, more twins and triplets from the womb being born right now than ever before. This is the time that we are living in today. We must consider the fact that we are being prepared to have an outpouring of the Holy Spirit where people get saved and healed. You will not want to go home from a service, you will want to hear more of God's Word, and you will want to worship for hours. God's glory will come in and you will get revelation and get healed, and no one will need to touch you. I saw this at the end times.

The end times are a little different than you storing water in your basement. We must be careful that we do not pack it up and hide in our bomb shelters when the whole idea is to bring in the harvest. The Lord of the harvest desires to bring in the harvest in the end days (see Matt. 9:38). That is what we are supposed to be doing. People in the world will start to see that God is with you, and it is not because of your good behavior. It is because you are adopted in as a family member of God, and God will start to live with you and work with you, and then you will know His ways.

I realized that for us to legitimately pray correctly, we have to be at the origin of everything and in the middle of everything. What does that mean? That means that where God thought of you and breathed you into your mother's womb is where you stand and give an account for your life, and where you start is where you end. He calls those things that are not as though they were (see Rom. 4:17). Jesus is the author and the finisher of your faith (see Heb. 12:2). The authorship and the finisher part of it are exactly the same spot. I have not moved in eternity; I have not moved an inch.

Chapter 6

YOU ARE A
KINGDOM AMBASSADOR

*But I have a greater witness than John's; for
the works which the Father has given Me
to finish—the very works that I do—bear
witness of Me, that the Father has sent Me.*

—JOHN 5:36

JESUS WAS LOOKING RIGHT AT ME, AND HE SAID,
"Kevin, you are not down here surviving, you are down
here preparing to rule and reign with Me for eternity,
shoulder to shoulder." When Jesus said that, I looked into

His eyes, and He said, "This is your proving ground for your position in eternity." At that very moment, I looked down at myself, and I was robed in rose gold. It was an ambassador's outfit. I am on probation for my next position. If I am faithful to do what I am doing now on this earth, then I move right into my next position. If you continue to be faithful and do what you are doing and let the Spirit of God mature you, then you will not have to sit in class in Heaven. You do not want to waste your time down here on earth because you are a kingdom ambassador.

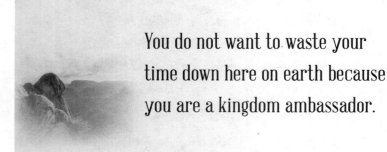

You do not want to waste your time down here on earth because you are a kingdom ambassador.

The ministry that God gave me is based on my relationship with Him because my position is still forward-looking. I am going to be in a position where I will have a lot of angels under me, and I will be over countries and territories because I qualified for that in this life. As we continue on in Christ, we are always going to have a position and a job in the heavenly realms. Everyone thinks that the Book of Revelation is a timeline, but it is not a timeline. It is a bunch of flashes of revelation that was given to John and Daniel and all the prophets. They had flashes, but it is not linear, it is not like a timeline, and you cannot look at it like that. There will be a period of time when we are going to be over other human beings. There will be a millennial reign for a thousand years (see Rev. 20:1-3). People are going to populate the earth for a thousand years, and satan will not be allowed to roam and tempt people until the very end of it. In the end, satan will be unleashed for a short time.

We read in the Book of Revelation that the New Jerusalem, all 1,500 square miles of it, will come down out of Heaven onto the Middle East (see Rev. 21:2). Israel should have had all that land and all that oil, but satan has reduced its area to the size of New Jersey. The New Jerusalem is going to set down there, and the earth will repopulate it, and we will rule over it (see Rev. 21:10-26).

ETERNAL LIFE, NOW!

You have to get ready to live your eternal life now. I am not waiting for eternal life because eternal life is in me, and it is in you. I am not going to try to find my borders by running into them. The Lord Jesus Christ has defined our borders for us, and He has told us, "You are going to rule and reign in this life as kings" (see Rev. 5:10) and *"everyone who has left houses or brothers or sisters or father or mother or wife or children or lands, for My name's sake, shall receive a hundredfold, and inherit eternal life"* (Matt. 19:29). You will receive a hundredfold and persecutions in this life on earth, so I have started to live my eternal life down here.

I have already died, and Jesus told me I did, and He sent me back. I am not afraid to die because I have already done that, and now I am going to live. Once the crucified life is established in your life and you realize what the crucified life is, then you can live. You must die to self (see Matt. 16:24-25). Jesus told me, "My people want resurrection power, but they do not want to die." He said, "You cannot have resurrection unless you have death" (see Rom. 6:1-11). Jesus told me to teach the crucified life, and I thought that was not going to go over very well. No one wants to hear about denying yourself and carrying your own cross, but that is the way it is supposed to be for a Christian, and it is to empower you.

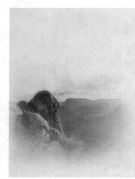

No one wants to hear about denying yourself and carrying your own cross, but that is the way it is supposed to be for a Christian, and it is to empower you.

Death brings you right to resurrection, because when you are baptized and you go under the water, you are buried with Christ through baptism into death. When you come up out of the water, just as Christ was raised from the dead, God immediately resurrects you to new life in Him through faith. The water of baptism represents the Jordan River. Everyone who came out of Egypt had to go through the Jordan River to get into the Promised Land, and it was a type and shadow of what was to come. That was why Jesus told John to baptize Him in order to fulfill all righteousness (see Matt. 3:15). Jesus had to go through everything we go through, and He had to go through the Jordan also, by going under the water and coming up. The Jordan represents the crucified life, and after you come up you can go right into the Promised Land.

You should just decide right now that you want to live eternally. When you die, you get promoted because, in actuality, there is no death. You die, and your body goes back into the earth where it belongs because that is where it originated—from the dust of the earth. In Heaven, you receive another body, and I received that body. I saw my new body, and I saw the uniform I was clothed in.

In my mind, I learned the ways of God by thinking this way. I am a supernatural being in a body, and I will live forever; I will never cease to exist. I will never be God, and so I am not even going to try. God is always right, and I am wrong, and that is fine with me. Whatever God says goes, and I am fine with that. I am not going to fight God because I am wasting time when I do so.

ADVANCING THE KINGDOM REALM

The whole idea of being a kingdom ambassador is that you have to settle it in your heart that you are not down here surviving; you are down here taking over territory for God. The Kingdom of God is advancing at an alarming rate. It is so powerful when you hook up with it, but you have to pay the price. Even when you are immersed in the overwhelming atmosphere of God, you realize your lack.

You are not down here surviving; you are down here taking over territory for God.

I surround myself with people who know how to get hold of God and do it right, and they are not in it for the wrong reason. I surround myself with those kinds of people, and then the atmosphere causes me to grow. When I grow in the Lord, then the devil gets bug-eyed because he sees that it is not to his advantage to even touch me or come at me. The devil attacking me will only push me further into the glory, and I come out bigger and fiercer.

And the Father Himself, who sent Me, has testi-fied of Me. You have neither heard His voice at any time, nor seen His form. But you do not have

His word abiding in you, because whom He sent,
Him you do not believe.

—JOHN 5:37-38

Jesus was talking about Himself here. He was saying that
the Jews did not discern who He was, and they mistreated
Him because they were not part of what God was doing. Jesus
was saying that the Word that was testifying of Him through
the prophets was not in them. They did not have God's Word
abiding in them so they could not hear God's voice, and they
did not believe what Jesus was saying. There are goats, and
there are sheep; there are tares, and there is wheat. Jesus told
me that I was no longer to try to convert a goat into a sheep.

Elijah was walking through a field, and the Lord told him
to take off his mantle and put it on a man who was plowing in
the field (see 1 Kings 19:19-20). Elijah walked by, and without
saying a word, he put his cloak on the man and kept walking.
The man, Elisha, ran after Elijah and asked if he could say
goodbye to his parents. Elijah answered and said, "What have
I done to you?" Elijah knew what he had done to Elisha, but
he knew that Elisha did not know because if Elisha knew he
would not have said a word and he would have followed Elijah.

Why did the disciples leave their boats, their wives, and
their children? Why did they drop their nets and start following Jesus? What kind of power did Jesus have? What
made those men who had businesses walk away? Jesus looked
at the huge crowds following Him, and He knew that the
reason they were following Him was that they had been fed

supernaturally and they had seen all the miracles. Those were the two wrong reasons to follow Him, according to Jesus.

As ambassadors of the Kingdom, we have to give out the Bread of life, the Word of life. We do not seek after miracles because miracles, signs, and wonders confirm and follow the preaching of the Word of God. If the Word of God is not being preached, you are not going to have signs and wonders following, because the signs and wonders follow the preaching of the Word. We do not operate in signs and wonders first. We preach the Word, and the giving out of the Bread of life causes people to change.

We do not operate in signs and wonders first. We preach the Word, and the giving out of the Bread of life causes people to change.

When Jesus talked about eating His flesh and drinking His blood (see John 6), He was talking about communion. He was saying, "You have to eat of Me." When Jesus said this to the crowd, He knew that many of them would be offended and leave because they were carnal. They did not discern who Jesus was. They did not hear Jesus' words; they only saw the miracles and were fed.

As ambassadors, we have got to break the Bread of life and hand it out. You can do this everywhere. It can be in the Bible study that you start at your house. It can be when you go to church and you offer to do something. You must constantly give out from your storehouse, and God will supply you. God's way is that you feed the people the Word of God, and transformation comes from the Word that is from Heaven. That Word comes to a minister who yields to the Spirit and gives forth Bread from Heaven. That is the way it is because it is the Word of God, and the Word is also the Spirit, and so it is not merely words.

> *You search the Scriptures, for in them you think you have eternal life; and these are they which testify of Me. But you are not willing to come to Me that you may have life.*
> —JOHN 5:39-40

In this verse, Jesus is speaking of people who search the Scriptures and think that they have found eternal life through them. They do not understand that these Scriptures testify of Jesus. It is the person of Jesus who is the Word; it is not just Scriptures. I can win an argument with the most violent sinner, and I will win an argument with them about God and Scripture, but they will still go to hell. I have won an argument, but I have lost because the goal was to bring people into the Kingdom.

I must win people over, and not by winning an argument because then I have not won. I do not argue with people because you do not win if they are in hell, screaming, and I do not want that for anyone, even my worst enemy. I do not even want witches to go to hell, who are workers of iniquity. They need to repent of their witchcraft and come into the Kingdom of God and then tell us all of the secrets of the enemy so that we can nail him. We are representing Jesus as an ambassador, so when we give out the Word of God we are portioning Jesus out to others. The Spirit of God is giving revelation through the words that we speak to the people.

> *I do not receive honor from men. But I know you, that you do not have the love of God in you. I have come in My Father's name, and you do not receive Me; if another comes in his own name, him you will receive. How can you believe, who receive honor from one another, and do not seek the honor that comes from the only God? Do not think that I shall accuse you to the Father; there is one who accuses you—Moses, in whom you trust. For if you believed Moses, you would believe Me; for he wrote about Me. But if you do not believe his writings, how will you believe My words?*
> —JOHN 5:41-47

You have to remember this is what Jesus said about Himself and what He faced in ministry. It is also what we will face in this life. This Scripture speaks of your life and ministry while you are in this world. As you read this verse, you can see the disconnect that these people had. Jesus was standing before them, and He was the fulfillment of everything that was ever written, and they did not receive Him. Remember, there are goats and sheep, and there are tares and wheat. The religious people will come at you, but the people who need help, who are poor and needy will listen to you because they are humble; they are not goats.

These humble people do not resist because they need and want help, and they are the people I am after. I am not going to sit and argue with a goat because they are a goat, and they are not going to convert. These kinds of people enjoy being a goat, and anything you say they will say exactly the opposite because they are contrary to you. They will always take the opposite view, and when you speak the Word they act as though it is only your opinion. They respond this way because it is what satan tells them; satan accuses the absolute truth of being an opinion.

ENGAGE WITH GOD

On the last day, that great day of the feast, Jesus stood and cried out, saying, "If anyone thirsts, let him come to Me and drink. He who believes in Me, as the Scripture has said, out of his heart will flow rivers of living water." But this He spoke concerning the Spirit, whom those believing in Him would receive; for the Holy Spirit was not yet given, because Jesus was not yet glorified.
—JOHN 7:37-39

Jesus was referring to the Holy Spirit here. He was explaining that after you eat His flesh and drink His blood, He will send the Holy Spirit to you, and you will begin drinking water that is from Heaven, who is the Holy Spirit. Paul said, "Do not be drunk with wine, which is excess, but be filled, drunk with the Holy Spirit" (see Eph. 5:18). Everything related to this dispensation—the outpouring of the Holy Spirit, speaking in tongues, fire, and prophecy—these are the four things that happened on the day of Pentecost. Jesus told His followers to wait for the baptism of the Holy Spirit to come, and while they were gathered together in one accord, the Holy Spirit came. God does not change, and His ways are established forever. *"I am the Lord, I change not"* (Mal. 3:6 KJV).

On the day of Pentecost, the same Holy Spirit that is inside of you came to Jesus' followers in Jerusalem (see Acts 2). The Holy Spirit came with a mighty rushing wind. There was fire on their heads, and they began to speak in other tongues. Then they began to speak in other languages that were not their own. A multitude of people from all the nations had come to Jerusalem because it was the day of the great feast. They heard their own languages being spoken. They knew these people were not from their country. Peter stood up, and he said, *"These are not drunk, as you suppose...But this is what was spoken by the prophet Joel"* (Acts 2:15).

Two thousand years later, the same Holy Spirit is in you. When was the last time the wind, the fire, the utterance, and the drunkenness came upon you? It is the same Word and the same Spirit. What has happened to us that we have become so sophisticated? Sometimes it takes a while for people to yield to the Spirit of God in the new wine, in the fire, and in the wind. Why is that? I believe that our culture and our exposure have caused us not to accept the move of the Spirit of God.

You know that the Holy Spirit is a person. He is not a bird. The Holy Spirit looks and acts like Jesus, and He makes you bold. He wants to frame your world, but it is based on the plans that are written in your book in Heaven. You need to fire your architect and let God be your architect. The Holy Spirit has a plan for your life. He is going to start moving you into what you are supposed to be doing. Yield to Him because this is the plan of your Father God whose face is shining upon you right now; He is smiling, and He is favoring you.

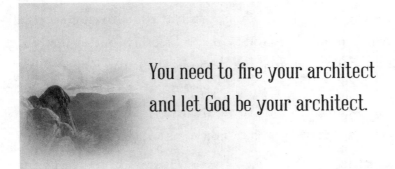

You need to fire your architect and let God be your architect.

If you yield, the Holy Spirit will frame your world, and He will say that this is the way it is going to be from now on. Then all of your friends will need to decide if they like you or not because they are not sure if they like you anymore. They will want the old friend back, but that friend is gone.

The powers of the coming age will come in because the Holy Spirit wants to rule and reign.

A SEASON OF PERFECT VISION

Are you ready for the year of perfect vision? It is coming to the church, and you are going to see as you have never seen before. You are going to be able to see through everything. I have been waiting for this season for years. One visit from the Holy Spirit, one visit from an angel, will shift a whole generation, and I want to be part of that. I want to be part of what God is doing. I saw in Heaven that I could not lose.

When I met Jesus, I realized that He was not one religion or another as far as the denomination is concerned. There is no one except Jesus whom you can come through to the Father. I found that God is always stepping out of the box, and He has shown me that demonic influence is real in the life of a Christian. Why am I getting words from the Lord for Christians who want to cut themselves or commit suicide? This kind of activity is real, and we cannot look the other way.

I needed a pastor when I was growing up, and I did not have one. I had someone who was a hireling who never told me that I needed to be born again. He had told me that if I joined the church, I would go to Heaven. I asked him about tithing and how it says, "Test Me in this" (see Mal. 3:10), and he told me not to test God; he had no answer for me. I want to help people and not look the other way when things are going on with them and say, "Well, you know that doesn't fit into what I believe, so it does not exist." This type of thinking does not make it go away. Your ability to discern must be operating at its highest in the days to come. The greatest move of God that has ever hit this earth is going to be at the end of this age, and it has started. It is going to start filling up the rooms everywhere. Every church, every prayer meeting, and everywhere you go will be filled to capacity.

The greatest move of God that has ever hit this earth is going to be at the end of this age, and it has started.

I have met people who have "never been wrong." I was on an airplane once, and there was a business lady. She wanted to put her suitcase where it was not allowed. If I had allowed it, I could have been fined. I said to her, "You cannot do that." When I told her that, it must have been the first time she had ever been told "no." You had to see that look. The universes started colliding, and all of a sudden you could feel this big hole was opening up, and you feel like you are going to fall into it. When that happened, I realized that there are degrees of influence on people's minds and who they are as a person.

Some people wrap themselves up in themselves. They are around people who automatically give them attention and pamper them and have everything catered to them. When someone does not treat them the way they have become accustomed to, that person must be wrong. They never stop to think that they are wrong, and maybe they are supposed to be a servant.

> *But he who is greatest among you shall be your servant.*
> —MATTHEW 23:11

The Word of God comes forth as truth, and in that truth you either have to fall on that rock, or the rock falls on you (see Matt. 21:44). Either you judge yourself, or you are going to be judged (see 1 Cor. 11:31-32). Jesus wants us to judge ourselves by the Word, and His personality is the Word. When I met Him, I realized that I was not all that I thought I was. When I came back to the earth, I came back with a degree of humility that I do not know how I could have obtained before I went. There is an element of pride in a person that needs to be burned out; you cannot receive from Heaven with pride.

> *And in a similar way, the Holy Spirit takes hold of us in our human frailty to empower us in our weakness. For example, at times we don't even know how to pray, or know the best things to ask for. But the Holy Spirit rises up within us to super-intercede on our behalf, pleading to God with emotional sighs too deep for words.*
> —ROMANS 8:26 TPT

Paul said that in our weakness, the Holy Spirit is going to come in and empower us to pray perfect prayers. Sometimes corporately, we all agree to pray in tongues, knowing that there is not going to be an interpretation because we are all speaking to God. In my limited human ability to pray effectively, I can only do so much in my own language. I have to yield to the Spirit so that I can pray mysteries.

YOU ARE THE CATALYST

I had two friends recently who were very sick. Both of these men are ministers of the Gospel. If I get into the soulish realm and the drama realm, then I have been diminished to where I am no good. My saltiness has been lost, and then I cannot be effective for my friends. I cannot attach myself emotionally to what is going on. The Lord told me not to call one of them until the timing was right for me to prophesy to him. The Lord said, "If you are not going to prophesy in faith, then you should not call him." It took a week or two for me to get into a place with the Lord that I was able to prophesy.

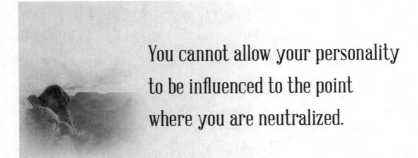

You cannot allow your personality to be influenced to the point where you are neutralized.

You cannot allow your personality to be influenced to the point where you are neutralized. You have to be the person who stands firm. How many have been in the position where you need a leader and no one wants to step forward? You just need one leader, just one, and nobody wants to do it. Then when someone does come forward, everybody will try to control that person and criticize them.

Everyone says that they want God, and it is the same way with me, but I am telling you that there is a veil, there is this shell that has to be broken in all of us. When we have a Holy Spirit meeting at our house, you are not able to walk to your car. Why is that? It is just my wife and me, but the power of God is so strong in the house that everyone who comes does not want to leave. That is not because we are special; it is because something happened to us that has nothing to do with getting on a plane, going to a hotel, and going to a meeting. God comes to us. We are *sent,* we are not *"went."* We are created in God's image, and we are created to have fellowship with Him, and it has to do with His ways.

When God comes in, He wants to be Himself, but God, Himself, is going to lay you out. There is going to be fire in His eyes, and the fire is going to come through His mouth, and you are going to catch on fire, and then the wind is going to blow. The devils have to be pushed out so that you can be released into this realm, and then there has to come a point where you enter into that realm. For that to happen, we have to engage God in spiritual activity, which means that we must intercede. You may ask, "Why do we have to intercede if God already knows everything?" Moses still had to walk up that mountain, and one of those times he walked up and the glory of God rested as a cloud, but he was not permitted to proceed, and he was made to wait. God made Moses stand there waiting for seven days, and then a voice came out of the cloud and told Moses he could come in (see Exod. 24:15-18).

If God's Spirit wants to intercede through you, then that is what you do. If you do not intercede, then something that was going to happen in the will of God will not happen. If you are a musician and the Holy Spirit tells you to play certain notes in a row, then that combination of notes will unlock something in the Spirit. It is the same thing with intercession. If you are supposed to intercede, pray, and get together, then that is what you need to do. What causes things to happen and break in the Spirit is that there is a catalyst, but God names the catalyst. God names the catalyst for that move of God, and the catalyst is the breaking point; it is the initiator of that next move of God.

God names the catalyst for that move of God, and the catalyst is the breaking point; it is the initiator of that next move of God.

There was a revival in Argentina that began many years ago that is still going on to this day. If you go to Argentina, you will have to wait in a line that goes around the block to get into the building. It all began when the people started meeting together, and they were praying and fasting, and they said that you could feel the power of God strongly in the meetings. They continued getting together and praying, and the power of God got stronger. Their tears were all over the floor and flowing down like rain. You could feel the angels in the room, and still there was no breakthrough. Finally, a man got up and said, "What has God said to one of you, and you have not done it?" This little lady said, "It is me. Three weeks ago, the Lord told me to go up there and slap that communion table." The man said, "Well, do it!" When she did, the power of God was released at that very moment, and that was how the revival started. That slap was the catalyst that started the revival.

Moses had to go to the mountain, he had to go to the burning bush, and he had to go to Pharaoh. Elijah had to slap the water with his mantle, and Elisha had to take the mantle and say, "Where is the God of Elijah?" Elisha had to strike the water with the mantle for the water to split and allow him to cross. Moses had to go down and put his staff in the water, and it split. Elijah had to put the water on the altar when he was going against the prophets of Baal. There are many more examples that teach us the ways of God. We need to start implementing them. There is a catalyst to the next move of God. If you saw how many angels are ready and waiting, you would want to start to engage the Lord for revival right now.

You might not know it unless I tell you, but you should know it because there are more with us than there are against us. Those angels are ready to go, and they are ready to engage in the entrance into your next phase in the Lord.

Those angels are ready to go, and they are ready to engage in the entrance into your next phase in the Lord.

My spirit is not limited by this realm. You need to have the faith of Abraham, which means that you could go and leave everything because the voice of God has told you to go. When you do not even question where you are going, that is the faith of Abraham. Scripture commends individuals for having great faith. Hebrews 11:27 tells us that they saw Him who is invisible. We would call that an oxymoron because how can you see something that is invisible? But if your spiritual eyes have been opened, you will see the invisible.

COMPLETING THE RACE

"Let not your heart be troubled; you believe in God, believe also in Me. In My Father's house are

many mansions; if it were not so, I would have told you. I go to prepare a place for you. And if I go and prepare a place for you, I will come again and receive you to Myself; that where I am, there you may be also. And where I go you know, and the way you know." Thomas said to Him, "Lord, we do not know where You are going, and how can we know the way?" Jesus said to him, "I am the way, the truth, and the life. No one comes to the Father except through Me."

—JOHN 14:1-6

You have permission to be who you are in Christ because God loves you. Jesus Christ Himself personally has invested in you, and He is very well aware of who you are. He has no problem handling and managing everyone because He is not bound by the laws that we are bound by down here. Jesus does not even need a secretary because He can keep rewinding the tape and entering into your world and keep doing that until you get it, and no time has passed by.

You have not lost any time, and you have not lost anything that was already gained. Your life before you is the entrance into eternity. You do not have to die physically to encounter eternal life. It is a well of water that is inside of you that wells up into eternal life. You stay full of the Spirit all the time. You used to be full of the devil, so why can't you now be full of the Spirit? You gave your body and your mind over to the devil, and you wasted portions of your life. What if you gave yourself over to the Spirit? Isn't it about time to give the Holy Spirit His due season? His due time?

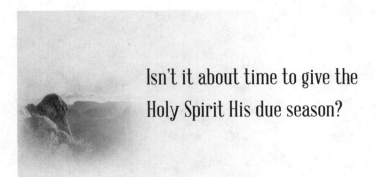

Isn't it about time to give the Holy Spirit His due season?

Remember, one day you will walk in the garden again with God. You will walk with Him in eternity, you will be with Him, and all will be well. You will have finished your race, and you won! You did it! I know this because I have already encountered it. I was in my future, and I saw everyone who has ever existed who made it to Heaven, assembled and worshiping the Lamb. I have been in your future, and it is very bright, and I saw that we all make it. I was sent back as a voice to speak to the people and bring you into the fullness of what Jesus Christ has bought for you. You can have it now, and you do not have to wait.

Chapter 7

HEAVEN IS YOUR HOME

If you love Me, keep My commandments. And I will pray the Father, and He will give you another Helper, that He may abide with you forever.

—JOHN 14:15-16

WHEREVER I GO IN THE WORLD, EVERY Christian I meet is on the same page. Whatever church I am in, I feel I can walk in and start talking, and I feel like I am with family. I never feel like I have to break the ice or anything like that. It is really great to meet pastors and people all over the world whom the Lord has educated in the Word of God. God has taught them how to move in the Spirit and how to live the Christian life. All over the world, the people there are on fire, and they fill the buildings. People are so ready for whatever God is going to do next.

> *The Spirit of truth, whom the world cannot receive, because it neither sees Him nor knows Him; but you know Him, for He dwells with you and will be in you.*
>
> —JOHN 14:17

I was recently in Australia, and it is the same way; the power of God is so strong over there. While we were visiting, Australia had an election, and the same exact thing that happened here in the U.S. happened there. The polls said that it was ten to one against the Spirit-filled president, and at 8:30 P.M. that night, the vote turned in his favor. While I was preaching, they notified everyone that he had won. The next day there were pictures of him in the news going to church with his family and speaking in tongues, and now the whole country is on fire for the Lord. Just like here in the states, they cannot understand what happened there, but God does. I am so encouraged by what I have seen over the last two and a half years.

I worked for Southwest Airlines for almost 30 years until I retired. It was never my idea to do that career in the first place. I was already in the ministry before the Lord had led me to work at Southwest, but it was a good time for me because I learned a lot. I had many good friends there who were strong Christian people. I remember thinking that someday the Lord is going to let me write a book about what happened to me in Heaven, and I am going to be allowed to talk about it. By faith, I would go to clothing stores, and I would buy a tie and a shirt. I know no one wears ties anymore, but I am on TV a lot, and I do not want to be like everybody else. On Wall Street, they come in wearing suits, and heads of businesses wear suits, and I have waited 30 years for this, so I want to dress for the part that the Lord has called me to do.

Jesus said to me, "I am sending you to make disciples of all nations, not just converts." In biblical times, a disciple was someone who was taught by a *rabbi*, the Hebrew word for teacher. They taught and had their students follow them around. Their followers would call them rabbi or teacher, but the word *disciple* comes from the word *discipline*. The students were to submit to the disciplines of the teacher. The disciples were being prepared to carry on what the rabbi was doing.

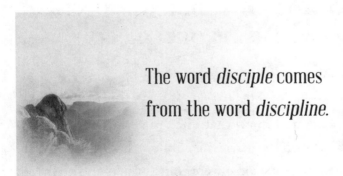

The word *disciple* comes
from the word *discipline*.

As a Christian, I found that we are not here to listen to a good talk or possibly get hit by the Lord, fall on the floor, and have someone carry us out. That is a nice experience to have, but when I met Jesus I found out that He was much more interested in our character. He was talking to me about character more than He was talking to me about comfort. There are times when you are not comfortable, but you *are* in the will of God. I think that things like that need to be taught because it is not always easy down here because there is a war.

> *Therefore you now have sorrow; but I will see you again and your heart will rejoice, and your joy no one will take from you. And in that day you will ask Me nothing. Most assuredly, I say to you, whatever you ask the Father in My name He will give you. Until now you have asked nothing in My name. Ask, and you will receive, that your joy may be full.*
>
> —John 16:22-24

No More Discouragement and Disappointment

When I went into the ministry, I became a teacher, and then I became the president of our School of Ministry called Warrior Notes, and I knew that I had to tell people the truth about what I saw on the other side. I knew that I had to create an atmosphere where people were transformed and changed, not just having an experience. I would have experiences and encounters and then they would fade away, and I found myself waiting for the next encounter. When I was in Heaven, the Lord showed me that we are not supposed to live from experience to experience or dose to dose of the power of God. We are supposed to yield and walk in the power of God constantly. It seemed so far away from me at the time, but I knew that absolute truth in Heaven is what we have to believe in, even if we do not experience it.

And He said to me, "My grace is sufficient for you, for My strength is made perfect in weakness." Therefore most gladly I will rather boast in my infirmities, that the power of Christ may rest upon me.

—2 CORINTHIANS 12:9

We are not supposed to live from experience to experience or dose to dose of the power of God. We are supposed to yield and walk in the power of God constantly.

God would say something, and it may be the exact opposite of what you have been encountering. You may not see any of what God says happening in your life. That is exactly when you should get excited, because God never asks you to do something you *can* do. God asks you to rely on Him in your weakness, and then He makes you strong. The apostle Paul taught about this, and Paul was excited about his weaknesses.

He said, "I am glad to boast about my weaknesses, so that the power of Christ can work through me" (see 2 Cor. 12:9).

> *Likewise the Spirit also helps in our weaknesses.*
> *For we do not know what we should pray for as we*
> *ought, but the Spirit Himself makes intercession*
> *for us with groanings which cannot be uttered.*
> —ROMANS 8:26

Paul said that the Holy Spirit comes in our weakness, not in our strength. He comes in our weakness and lifts us up and causes us to pray the perfect will of God under the influence of the Holy Spirit. You have to learn to know where you end and where God begins in every situation in your life every day. You have to yield yourself to the ministry of the Holy Spirit every day. I did die on the operating table, and each day for me is a gift. Each breath I take is a gift because I remember getting out of my body on the operating table and walking around the room and not being able to get back into my body. It is an amazing feeling when you have no more control over your life and God owns you. My destiny was sealed; I could not get back into my body. I was looking at my body on the operating table and I tried to think of everything that I knew. I already had a degree in theology, but it was not going to help me now because I was out of control. I learned through this experience how both realms work.

Down here, the weaknesses that we experience are because this world has fallen. You can ask someone to do something, and they are only thirty-six inches from your mouth, but they will not go and do what you asked. Sometimes they come back and ask you what you just said. How can thirty-six inches mess up what you just said? It is a broken world. Things are not always reliable because the world is broken, and it is not the way it was when God made it.

I saw when I was in Heaven that everything is perfect, and it has always been perfect. In Heaven, they do not have the limitations that we have down here. Anyone who died and encountered Heaven would refuse to come back. You would not even know how you died because you are not told, and you forget what happened right before you died. I did not know what happened, and no one ever explained it to me. I was being promoted, and everybody was celebrating.

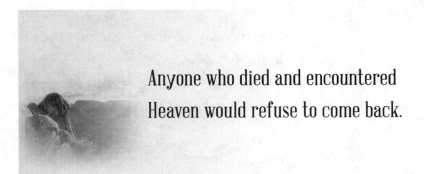

Anyone who died and encountered Heaven would refuse to come back.

It is a big celebration for a Christian to go to Heaven, but over there everything is perfect and there are no limitations. Jesus will allow you to look back at your life and look at the world, and you will see it clearly for the first time. You will see Jesus clearly, and all the situations of your life, and you will realize that you were never made for a broken world. The way that God created man, in the beginning, was in His image.

In Heaven, there are no such things as *dis*-appointments; there are only appointments, and you do not have *dis*-couragement; you have courage. These things evade us down here, and you have to build yourself up to be encouraged, and you have to tell yourself you can make it. You have to tell yourself that people do appreciate you even when they are sticking their tongue out at you or worse. You have to be on your game all the time down here and feel the pressure. The way that God created man was to live in a perfect world.

When you are born again, your spirit is restored back to God's original intent. When you pray, you expect God to answer you immediately, and when you see someone in a wheelchair, you want to yank them out of it and say, "Be healed and walk in Jesus' name." The reason you feel that way is because your spirit knows God's will for everyone. There are people who, through no fault of their own, were born that way. They were born that way because the world is corrupt, and it is not fair.

In this world, there are limitations placed on you, and it is just not fair. In the perfect world where Jesus Christ lives and dwells and that He made for us in Heaven, everything is perfect. You are going to have a beautiful home up there, and everything is going to be exactly the way you want it. Any children who have passed away early all go straight to Heaven and are waiting for you there.

And God will wipe away every tear from their eyes; there shall be no more death, nor sorrow, nor crying. There shall be no more pain, for the former things have passed away.

—REVELATION 21:4

There were a lot of children in Heaven, and they were playing at the River of Life, and they were waiting for their parents to come to Heaven. The Lord God was holding them there at a certain age so that when their parents came, they could encounter the child growing up with them. God the Father can do whatever He wants, and He makes it so that everyone gets paid back for anything terrible that they encountered down here. God takes all of your tears away.

But without faith it is impossible to please Him, for he who comes to God must believe that He is, and that He is a rewarder of those who diligently seek Him.

—HEBREWS 11:6

God takes all of your tears away.

God is a rewarder of those who diligently seek Him, and He is keeping track of everything. Anything you do down here is going to be kept track of, and you get a reward for it. Failure is not even an option in Heaven. The angels that are sent to help you never think that you are going to fail. No one in Heaven thinks you are going to fail. They all love you; they are all voting for you, and they are cheering for you.

> *I will praise You, for I am fearfully and wonder-*
> *fully made; marvelous are you works, and that my*
> *soul knows very well.*
>
> *—PSALM 139:14*

Everyone in Heaven wants you to finish up your race down here with joy and let God wrap this age up because that is what He wants to do. Everything you are going through down here is very frustrating, but it is because you are a very complicated being—ask your friends. We are very intricately made; we are fearfully and wonderfully made.

Chapter 8

PARTNERING WITH GOD

*But the Lord said to him, "Go, for he is a
chosen vessel of Mine to bear My name before
Gentiles, kings, and the children of Israel."*
—ACTS 9:15

ABRAHAM DID IT, MOSES DID IT, AND ANYONE WHO
ever did anything with God partnered with Him.
Partnering means that you connect with someone
and you say, "Whatever you are doing, I am going to do." I
find someone above me and I partner with them; I covenant
with people above me because I get everything that they get.
When two or more are gathered together in Jesus' name, He
is there in the midst of them (see Matt. 18:20). When Jesus

is in your midst, He said that whatever we agree on we will have it (see Matt. 18:19). There are no limitations written here. Jesus also said, "Ask and you shall receive, seek, and you shall find, knock, and the door shall be opened for you" (see Matt. 7:7-8). There are no disclaimers between any of these things that Jesus said. Nothing is limiting you. There is no fine print in Heaven; it is all in big print, and everything is all out in the open.

Nothing is limiting you. There is no fine print in Heaven; it is all in big print, and everything is all out in the open.

God is the All-Sufficient One, and if God does not have what you are asking from Him, He will make it for you. He will cause it to come, and it is no big deal. You have to find out what track God has you on and do what He is calling you to do. If you are going to flow with the Spirit and receive from Heaven; you are going to do what God asks you to do. It might be just picking up the donkey jawbone like Samson and swinging or it might be just having that staff in your hand that you cannot explain why it turns into a snake. What happened to Moses did not make any sense, but it was countercultural because the culture was not right. It is going counter to the system because the system is broken. You are not supposed to be gathering so that you can survive. You are supposed to be a distribution center. God has made you all-sufficient in Him, and if you adhere to that you will be completely taken care of in every area. When that happens, no one can control you.

Everything is set up with a debt system so that people have power over you. That is why God made gold, and He made it so that we cannot replicate it. God locked gold out of ever being replicated because it is based on His system in Heaven. When the United States made the gold standard, they were right on. Satan could not control people if we only printed enough money to represent how much gold we had. The United States government got us off the gold standard so they could float the dollar, which means that now they can print as much money as they want. The monetary system is set up so that you get stolen from and have to foot the bill.

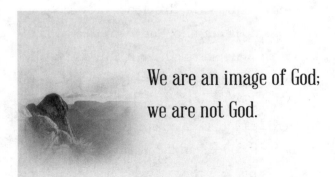

We are an image of God;
we are not God.

Just as God made the gold His, it was similar to what He did in the Garden of Eden. God said to Adam and Eve that the tree was His to eat from and that they could not eat from that tree. God could handle the knowledge of good and evil, but man could not. God made us in His image, but we are an image of God; we are not God. God knew that Adam and Eve could not handle knowing the difference between good and evil and still be able to choose good. We are made in God's image, but we are a replica, and we are not the exact copy. Just as you cannot replicate gold, God made us in a way that we cannot be replicated. There is a process in which God blocks certain things out. We are not to concentrate on the things that we are locked out of as Eve did. Eve was fixated on the fact that she was missing out by not eating of that tree in the garden, only she was not missing out. Eve did not need to know the difference between good and evil.

God is the All-Sufficient One, and He has made for Himself gold that you cannot replicate. God also has the ability to know good and evil and still choose good. Now because our eyes are open and we know the difference between good and evil, our weakness does not allow us to choose good all the time, and this is the struggle we have in our daily walk. What I saw in Heaven was that you must keep your focus on the All-Sufficient One every day because He is your source. You are never going to *be* God, but you can be *like* Him. God is always going to be your source, and you are always going to need Him, and He has made it that way. He has locked you out of being God.

The rich rules over the poor, and the borrower is servant to the lender.

—Proverbs 22:7

God is always going to be your source, and you are always going to need Him, and He has made it that way.

The system that is down here on earth is to fight for control. I have to tell people that they need to be delivered from this system and not allow themselves to be controlled, and I have to break that from people. You have to own everything. In other words, you have to get out of debt, and you have got to be the lender and not the borrower.

You will receive this blessing if you are careful to obey all the commands of the Lord your God that I am giving you today. The Lord your God will bless you as he has promised. You will lend money to many nations but will never need to borrow. You will rule many nations, but they will not rule over you.

—Deuteronomy 15:5-6 NLT

God is the All-Sufficient One. When God comes in and says, "No more poverty," then that is the way it is supposed to be. Prosperity in the Bible is used so many times it will make your head spin. It has never been God's plan for you to be poor. One denomination has made it a pillar of the church to be poor. This kind of thinking comes from demonic influence. I am going to be effective in this generation, and the only way to do that is to speak the truth in love. I have to stand before the Lord Jesus Christ. I have already stood before Him, and I know that *He* is my reward. I have already received the reward because I got to spend time with Him, and He validated me. You too, are validated by Jesus because He can look at you face to face. However, in this world, we are going to have trouble (see John 16:33).

The hardest part for me is to get people to engage in the supernatural. They want the supernatural, but it is not something that occurs automatically. It is like that man who was waiting at the pool of Bethesda for the water to be stirred so that he could be healed (see John 5:1-15). An angel would randomly come down and stir the water, and the man was speaking to Jesus about it and he did not discern that Jesus, the Healer, was right before him. Jesus told me that this is a condition of the church right now. We are waiting for the waters to be stirred by a supernatural event when the Healer is right here. The man at the pool discerned Jesus as a helper, and he asked Jesus to help him get in when the water stirred. Jesus said to him, "Rise, take up your bed and walk." He had to partner with the Healer.

Jesus answered and said to her, "If you knew the gift of God, and who it is who says to you, 'Give Me a drink,' you would have asked Him, and He would have given you living water."

—JOHN 4:10

We are waiting for the waters to be stirred by a supernatural event when the Healer is right here.

Jesus was talking to the woman at the well, and He said, "Woman, if you knew who was standing before you." Jesus was right before her and would have given her living water. People do not discern who Jesus is, so they do not receive. The key is knowing that God is the All-Sufficient One if we are to partner with Him and receive from Heaven.

THE CHANGE YOU NEED IS IN HIM

But the Lord said to him, "Go, for he is a chosen vessel of Mine to bear My name before Gentiles, kings, and the children of Israel."

—ACTS 9:15

In this Scripture, the Lord was talking about the apostle Paul, and He was saying how Paul was a chosen vessel of the Lord's. The believers were all afraid of Paul because he was killing Christians. God can do miracles, and He can change people, and He can change you. I need change, but change comes through transformation when truth comes in, a living truth through the Holy Spirit, and then you have a living faith; you have a living relationship.

When I was in Heaven, I saw that Jesus was not a system or associated with any particular denomination. Jesus was *I Am,* and to be honest with you, none of the denominations were even close to who Jesus was, but they all served Him in the capacity of the revelation that was available. However, the world was made through His words.

> *I have been crucified with Christ; it is no longer I who live, but Christ lives in me; and the life which I now live in the flesh I live by faith in the Son of God, who loved me and gave Himself for me.*
>
> —GALATIANS 2:20

FAVOR IS NOT FAIR

If you are saved, born again, Spirit-filled, and you are walking with God, there is another step, and it is called favor. Favor is not fair to everyone else around you. If God favors you because you pleased Him so much, He might visit with you and take you with Him as He did with Enoch. God found Enoch irresistible, and God just took him away. Jesus explained this to me. He said that when you partner with God, you should say that your life is not your own anymore and that for the rest of your life, you are going to allow Jesus Christ to use your body to live out through you. What happens when you give yourself to the Lord is that people are going to get mad at you because everything about you is going to start to prosper. You are going to have favor.

If God favors you because you pleased Him so much, He might visit with you and take you with Him as He did with Enoch.

Except when there may be no poor among you; for the Lord will greatly bless you in the land which the Lord your God is giving you to possess as an inheritance.

—DEUTERONOMY 15:4

There shall be no poor among you; what is it in this verse that people do not understand? In an Old Testament Covenant, God said, "You are going to be the head and not the tail" (see Deut. 28:13). God said, "You are going to lend to many nations but not borrow" (see Deut. 15:6). It is so sad, and Jesus was hurt when I met Him because He had accomplished this amazing New Covenant, a better Covenant with better promises, and we choose to be poor. We choose to be sick and have demon problems, relationship problems, and the devil has shut so many of us down in all those areas. Yet the table is sitting there and has been set with bowls of healing. "Could you pass me the healing, please? I want another serving. I need a serving of that deliverance." Prosperity, health—these are all things that come from God, and God does not have any bad thing up there to give you.

> *Every good gift and every perfect gift is from above,*
> *and comes down from the Father of lights, with*
> *whom there is no variation or shadow of turning.*
>
> —JAMES 1:17

All good things come down from the Father of heavenly light. The problem with trusting and having faith is that we do not understand the personality of God. He does not have anything bad to give you. When Jesus came on the earth, He went around *"doing good and healing all who were oppressed by the devil"* (Acts 10:38). Jesus said, *"The thief does not come except to steal, and to kill, and to destroy. I have come that they may have life, and that they may have it more abundantly"* (John 10:10). It was enough to give you life, but Jesus said abundant life. There is a shift in your thinking and your heart because you realize that God is a good God and desires to favor you.

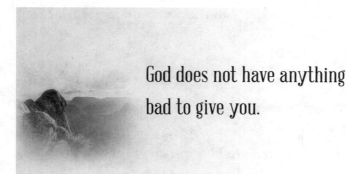

God does not have anything
bad to give you.

THE GOODNESS OF GOD

I can preach about hell, and I could scare hell out of you to the point that you will want to repent. I meet people all the time, and they have hell in them, and they are going to hell, and they are fine with it, but they are a mess, and I drive hell out. I am talking to them, and they are not saved, but hell is leaving them. The demons are leaving them, and their face is contorting. They are blinking and seeing flashes because the angels are coming, and all of a sudden the demons are leaving. They are not even saved yet, but they are free, and they start crying. I ask them for their hand. I tell them that the Lord is asking them for their life, and to pray with me. It happens because hell leaves them enough to where they can see the Gospel, and they want to partake of it.

Why, as Christians, do we not go to the table and eat of all the provision that is given to us? Why are we waiting until we get to Heaven to do this? We will not need that provision up there. We do not need prosperity or healing up there. While I am here, I am going to walk in the power of the resurrection. How about you?

> *According to the grace of God which was given to me, as a wise master builder I have laid the foundation, and another builds on it. But let each one take heed how he builds on it. For no other foundation can anyone lay than that which is laid, which is Jesus Christ. Now if anyone builds on this foundation with gold, silver, precious stones, wood, hay, straw, each one's work will become clear; for the Day will declare it, because it will be revealed by fire; and the fire will test each one's work, of what sort it is. If anyone's work which he has built on it endures, he will receive a reward. If anyone's work is burned, he will suffer loss; but he himself will be saved, yet so as through fire. Do you not know that you are the temple of God and that the Spirit of God dwells in you? If anyone defiles the temple of God, God will destroy him. For the temple of God is holy, which temple you are.*
> —1 CORINTHIANS 3:10-17

You do not hear about this Scripture much anymore. Paul was teaching this to the Corinthians 1,900 years ago, and during that time, Ananias and Sapphira lied to the Holy Spirit and fell dead in the church (see Acts 5:1-11). That was in a congregation of 5,000 people. We are going to have to apologize to Ananias and Sapphira because there are people in ministry who are doing worse things than that and are still living. People can get to a place where they are deluded.

Your faith, your trust in God, makes an environment where you live and you move and you have your being in Him; you have favor, and the demons know it (see Acts 17:28). Everything you put your hand to will prosper (see Deut. 30:9). We should not be worse off in the New Testament than the Old Testament. In the Old Testament, they believed that when they planted their crops and tended to their livestock, they would prosper.

Look at Abraham; God told him to leave his country as we saw before (see Gen. 12:1-3). A short time later, Scripture tells us that Abraham was very rich in livestock, in silver, and gold (see Gen. 13:2), and that was a result of partnering with God. God came to Abraham and said, *"I will make you a great nation"* (Gen. 12:2). God changed his name from Abram to Abraham and told him that he was going to be the father of everyone.

God took Abraham to the land that eventually became Israel. This account was how God began His relationship with Israel and how Abraham became our father. In the New Testament through Jesus, we have a better covenant, but we are still a part of the Covenant of Abraham because we have been grafted in (see Rom. 11:17-18). God continually brags about the faith of Abraham.

Under the New Covenant, the things that are written about you in Heaven would blow you away. If you saw the page that was written in Heaven for you just for today, you would fall on the floor. I could preach about hell and scare people into Heaven, or I could talk about the goodness of God and lead people into repentance. People need a revelation of the goodness of God, and they will want to repent.

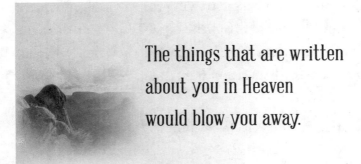

The things that are written about you in Heaven would blow you away.

I died, and Jesus took me to Heaven, and I wanted to stay there. The Lord said, "I can insert you back in, and I will let you remember what you saw, and what I told you, and then you tell everyone the truth, and you cannot fail." I did not want to come back, but Jesus told me that I *could not fail* if I do this. I was arguing with the Lord, and I said, "I am not going back to that; it is a mess."

Jesus had opened my eyes, and I saw everything the way it was, and I was not going back. Then Jesus said, "It is not about you. If you go back, I will reroute people. They will end up the right way instead of the wrong way. If you go back, you can change a whole generation, and you can change history. If I insert you back in, it will not end up the way it was going to be for many people." Then Jesus said, "You cannot fail; if you go back, you cannot fail, and I will make sure."

I had never heard anyone talk to me like this. I was looking at Him, and I knew it was Jesus, and I knew that He could not lie. Jesus said, "It is all extra credit if you go back because you have already been faithful, so you are done. But if you go back, it will be completely rigged in your favor, and all you have to do is show up before the people and talk. I will come, and I will tell you what to say, and when I am done talking, you are done talking, and you can get in your car and go."

It sounded pretty good, so I came back, and since that time that I came back there has been one supernatural event after another. Those events were not me as an apostle, or a prophet, or a pastor, or a teacher, or an evangelist, but as Kevin, a flight attendant who prays in tongues. Jesus told me not to talk about this for 23 years, so I did not. The minute I was released to talk about it, many things began happening. I wrote a book, I was on TV, and I started a School of Ministry.

What is it that is hidden from you that has to do with your trust? It has to do with you just adhering to Jesus Christ and making yourself available to live out the books that are written about you in Heaven. Not one child of God is insignificant, and if anyone is insignificant it is me. I consider myself less than you because I know so much now, and I am responsible for it. I would rather have not seen Jesus and lived by faith because once you get all this substance, you are accountable.

The demons do not want you to know what I am telling you. God has set it up; you can walk in power, and whatever you say goes, you should not hold back. In the privacy of my own home, I beat the daylights out of the devil all over the world. I pray for all my pastor friends in other countries. I pray for all my Facebook friends, YouTube subscribers, students in our School of Ministry, and every time someone gives to the ministry. Whenever someone gives to our ministry, I receive an alert on my phone, and I start praying for them. Why? Because it is all rigged in my favor.

God has set it up; you can walk in power, and whatever you say goes, you should not hold back.

Imagine someone dies, and they come back, and now they are not afraid to die anymore. That person can now see how much the devil has lied to them, and they know how big of a liar he is, and they can laugh at him. So, when the devil threatens to kill that person, their response has to be, "It is too late. I have already died; do you have anything else?" You start throwing it back at the devil, and before you know it, you can see him sweating. These demons get nervous because they do not know a lot of Christians like that.

The secret about demons is that demons do not have a plan B. They put everything on the table in a bet that you are going to believe everything they say the first time they say it. If you do not believe it and if you resist them and start laughing, it is the best thing you can do. You start laughing every time the devil talks to you or does anything to you. If you go out and you have a flat tire, start laughing and say, "That's all you got? You have got to be kidding me!"

I always wondered why the demons cried out when Jesus came to cast them out of the demon-possessed man of the Gergesenes (see Matt. 8:28-29). If the demons had kept their mouths closed, they would not have gotten cast out, but they started screaming at Jesus. The demons knew they would have to go, and they were trying to compromise with Jesus and negotiate a deal with Him so that they would not have to leave the area. These demons were disembodied spirits from before the flood. They lost their bodies and now roam the earth, and they are mad.

The devil is not red with horns and a pitchfork, but that is what he wants you to believe. The devil is a cherub that fell from Heaven, and the roaming spirits that you deal with here on earth once lived on this earth in the flesh. These spirits are hybrids, and they are not redeemable, and they hate you, but they have no power over you through Jesus Christ. You have to be rough with the devil, and you do that by *"Building yourselves up on your most holy faith, praying in the Holy Spirit, keep yourselves in the love of God"* (Jude 1:20-21).

You must command demons constantly and blame them for everything; even if they say they were not in the area, too bad. The devil is a liar. That is what I do because the devil needs to pay for what he has done. The devil is the thief that has been caught, and now he has got to pay back sevenfold and give up the substance of his house (see Prov. 6:30-31). It is payback time. When you wake up in the morning, you are a threat to the enemy, and he cannot do anything about it unless you let him.

When you wake up in the morning, you are a threat to the enemy, and he cannot do anything about it unless you let him.

Then Jesus called a little child to Him, set him in the midst of them, and said, "Assuredly, I say to you, unless you are converted and become as little children, you will by no means enter the kingdom of heaven. Therefore whoever humbles himself as this little child is the greatest in the kingdom of heaven."

—Matthew 18:2-4

Jesus taught people who had a third-grade education or less, and everything He said and taught was simple, and if it is complicated it is not Christianity. Jesus said that you must become like a little child to inherit the Kingdom of God. We enter in with a simple faith—Father God said it, and that is the way it is going to be. The power of the Holy Spirit is so strong and so willing, and Jesus said, *"The spirit indeed is willing, but the flesh is weak"* (Matt. 26:41). Our problem is in our trust. You must remember how good God is.

It brings you great joy every morning when you wake up and you know what God's will is for your life and that you are here to walk as Jesus did. I am not going to settle for the works of Jesus; I am settling for the greater works. I am settling for the fact that there is a new sheriff in town, and we are not going to do things the old way anymore. That is what I say every morning when I wake up. This is how I receive from Heaven. Again, I am just Kevin who is a Christian, who loves God, prays in tongues and beats up on the devil. You can be the same way. You can receive everything that Heaven has to offer you on this earth.

Every place my wife and I have ever lived, as soon as we move in, the city starts to repave the roads, change the signs, fill the potholes, and new buildings and new businesses come in. The first time it happened, we half-jokingly said that we wished they would fill that pothole on our street. The next thing we knew, there was a guy out there filling it in. We knew that we were on to something, so then every time we moved, we would pray in the Spirit and do warfare, and we would go there for a week and pray in tongues in our house. Every area we moved to began to improve. I realized that it was a trend, and I saw how important it was to know what is happening in the Spirit wherever you go.

In Heaven, Abraham wants to meet *you* because you were chosen to live at the end of the age. All the apostles and prophets built the foundation, but we get to live at the end of the age and wrap it up, and it does not matter where you live because you are significant. You ought to reconsider at what level your trust is, and that maybe you need to bring it up a notch and start receiving from God. When you call Amazon and tell them that you have not gotten your box, they will ask you if you opened your door because it has already been delivered and it is sitting right outside. It is already there, and I saw in Heaven that receiving from Heaven is that simple because it has already been delivered.

> *Grace and peace be multiplied to you in the knowledge of God and of Jesus our Lord, as His divine power has given to us all things that pertain to life and godliness, through the knowledge of Him who called us by glory and virtue, by which have been given to us exceedingly great and precious promises, that through these you may be partakers of the divine nature, having escaped the corruption that is in the world through lust.*
> —2 PETER 1:2-4

God has already given you all those things that you need for life and godliness through Jesus Christ, and they have already been delivered to you. Those precious promises that you have been given allow you to escape the corruption that is in the world caused by lust, and you can now be a partaker of the divine nature. So many miracles are about to occur in your life because it is a breakthrough anointing.

Chapter 9

RELATIONSHIP OF TRUST

*Now faith is the substance of things hoped
for, the evidence of things not seen. For by
it the elders obtained a good testimony.*

—HEBREWS 11:1-2

I REALIZED A FEW THINGS ABOUT FAITH WHILE I WAS
in Heaven that I did not understand when I was down
here, and I went to the best schools for faith. I heard this
phrase at school almost every day, "I am going to work the
Word," and it never sat right with me. When I met Jesus, He
was standing before me, and He *was* the Word, and when I
looked into His eyes, I thought, "I am not working Him; He

is working me." Those 45 minutes with the Lord revolutionized my thinking.

I only said a couple of things to Jesus during the 45 minutes I was with Him because I did not know everything that He knows. I know everything I know, so I was going to keep quiet because I did not need to spout off what I knew to Jesus. After all, He was not going to be impressed anyway. I needed to know what He knew, and that is the way I am. When I am around people who have been in ministry for 40 years, I do not speak; I let them talk. I do everything that my fathers, who are above me in the faith, tell me to do, and I salute them because they have been doing this for a long time, and I have not.

The perception that we have about faith could be wrong. The Hebrew way of thinking in the Old Testament about trust is the same as it is in the New Testament about faith. When I met Jesus, I saw that there was no difference between Jesus as a Person, who was standing before me, and what it was that He was saying. Who Jesus was as a Person and what He said were exactly the same.

Jesus never said anything different than who He was, and He was very careful to say exactly what He meant. He could create universes with His words because He has already. Many people picture Jesus as a weak person on a cross from all those paintings where He looks so feminine. I found that Jesus is very strong and has a very strong personality. I was shocked because Jesus is the best-looking person in the universe. That is the person I met.

By faith we understand that the worlds were framed by the word of God, so that the things which are seen were not made of things which are visible.

—HEBREWS 11:3

For assuredly, I say to you, whoever says to this mountain, "Be removed and be cast into the sea," and does not doubt in his heart, but believes that those things he says will be done, he will have whatever he says. Therefore I say to you, whatever things you ask when you pray, believe that you receive them, and you will have them.

—MARK 11:23-24

The Lord Jesus Christ said this: "If you believe in your heart what you say with your mouth, it shall come to pass, and you shall have that." That is the way that the worlds were formed. Everything that is made was made through Jesus Christ by His Word, and He framed the worlds with His Word.

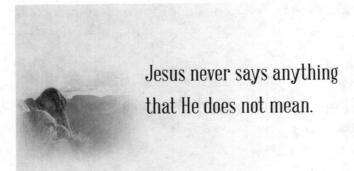

Jesus never says anything that He does not mean.

Jesus never says anything that He does not mean. He never says anything jokingly because Jesus said in Matthew 12:36 that you will be held accountable for every idle word that comes out of your mouth, but no one visits that. We skip over it. I was considered a scholar in theology, and I had to come back from the dead and go and look that up. When Jesus told me that Scripture chapter and verse and who He was saying it to, I had to go look it up because I did not believe Him. I did not even know that it was in the Bible.

What is faith? *"Faith is the substance of things hoped for, the evidence of things not seen"* (Heb. 11:1). Men of old were told to leave where they were and go to a place that would be designated when they got there (see Heb. 11:8). God just said, "Go," and He did not always tell people where they were going, and they went by faith. By faith they saw Him who was invisible (see Heb. 11:27), and by faith they were looking for a city whose builder and maker was God (see Heb. 11:10). These faith phrases are all found in Hebrews 11.

In your life, you have to become accustomed to being around a person who means what they say and who keeps their word. We are not accustomed to that because people will say something and then they do not do it. In Heaven, there is no difference between me and my word, because everyone up there is known by their word. There is no difference between who they are as a person and their word. In our life, the reason that we do not cooperate with Heaven in faith is that we are not familiar with people who keep their word.

Trust is knowing that God has said something and He surely will do it (see 1 Thess. 5:24). You may not be sure that God heard you when you prayed, but Jesus said, "Father, You always hear Me when I pray" (see John 11:42). Jesus was God's Son, but in Romans 8:15 it talks about us having received the Spirit of adoption and that we have been adopted into the family of God. We are now children of God, and we can be assured our Father in Heaven hears our prayers.

Paul says, "*The Spirit Himself bears witness with our spirit that we are children of God*" (Rom. 8:16). "*But as many as received Him, to them He gave the right to become children of God, to those who believe in His name*" (John 1:12). Creation is right now groaning that the sons of God would be revealed (see Rom. 8:19-21). Creation fell with us, and creation itself will be delivered from the bondage of corruption into the liberty of the sons of God.

THE AWESOME GOD WE SERVE

God has worked this amazing salvation for human beings. Jesus volunteered before the foundation of the world to come back, knowing that man would fall. Jesus was slain from the foundation of the world, according to the Book of Revelation (see Rev. 13:8). God made man in His own image; there was never a creation like man before. It was a liability for God to give man free will. God knew that He could lose man, and because of free will God let man fall. Jesus volunteered ahead of time to come to earth and buy us back. It sounds like it is all rigged, and it is. Paul killed Christians, and when he became saved he announced in his letters to the churches that he was set apart as an apostle from birth (see Gal. 1:15). He also said, "I have wronged no man" (2 Cor. 7:2). You know that before Paul knew the Lord, he had Stephen stoned to death (see Acts 7:58-59).

> *You saw who you created me to be before I became me! Before I'd ever seen the light of day, the number of days you planned for me were already recorded in your book.*
>
> —Psalm 139:16 TPT

The plan of God for your life was intact before you were born. There are books written about you, and each one of your days was written in a book before one of them came to pass.

> *You've gone into my future to prepare the way, and in kindness you follow behind me to spare me from the harm of my past. With your hand of love upon my life, you impart a blessing to me.*
>
> —Psalm 139:5 TPT

God goes into your future, paving the way for you with each step. God stands in your future, and then He goes behind you and protects you from the hurts of your past. That is the God you serve. God designed this all before we were born.

God goes into your future,
paving the way for you with
each step, and then He goes
behind you and protects you
from the hurts of your past.

We are getting to the place in time when the Lord wants to come back. God needs us to go and witness to everyone and tell them about the plan that God has for man, and it is that no one should go to hell. Hell was made for the devil and his angels, according to Jesus (see Matt. 25:41). Each one of us has a book written about us, and there are people in hell right now who have this beautiful book in Heaven written about them. Those in hell chose not to live out their book for whatever reason, but we do not have to be like the ones who faded back.

> *Let us therefore come boldly to the throne of grace,*
> *that we may obtain mercy and find grace to help*
> *in time of need.*
> —HEBREWS 4:16

We can be aggressive and go into the presence of God, and we can ask Him for help relying on the Holy Spirit, but it has to do with trust. You have to settle it once and for all that there is one person in the universe you can trust. Jesus

Christ, your Redeemer, the center of the universe, and the name above all names—He is good for His Word. If Jesus has said something to you, you can bank on it because it is going to happen. His Word is speaking all the time; you only have to open it. The Spirit of God is here to confirm and take you into a higher level of trust.

God has never failed anyone. Jesus broke down and cried when He told me what He went through for me. I want to make it worth His while because He said, "My people, they do not know what I have done for them. I have made them priests and kings of the Most High God. I have made them more than conquerors (see Rom. 8:37). I went ahead of them and destroyed the enemy, and I made him as nothing."

Faith is the title deed, the substance of things hoped for, and we have it. If I took out of my bag right now the title deed to my house and handed it to you, that is your house. What if you are here and my house is in New Orleans? It is still your house because I gave it to you, and you have the title deed even if you do not know what color the carpet is. If you know me, and if I gave you the title deed and I say that is your house, then that is your house because I am a man of my word. That is the way that God is, but how many times have you been promised things and they have not come to pass? It is because people are weak, but God is never weak.

The Spirit Confirms the Word

So then faith comes by hearing, and hearing by the word of God.

—Romans 10:17

We need to saturate our environment with the Word of God. We have to feed ourselves on the truth that was spoken of by holy men of old who were moved and wrote the Bible. The Holy Spirit moved on people, and they wrote the Bible by the inspiration of the Holy Spirit. The Spirit of God initiated what was written in the Bible, and then when you receive it He initiates the confirmation in your life. The Spirit always comes in to confirm God's Word because it is eternal. It does not matter whether you believe it or not, because it does not change what God believes and what He has already said.

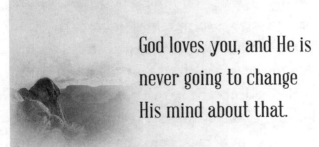

God loves you, and He is never going to change His mind about that.

God loves you, and He is never going to change His mind about that. God had already proven that He loves you before you were born because He wrote a book about you. If you throw out Psalm 139, what is the next psalm that you will have to throw out? Then what is the next book of the Bible that you would have to toss out? You say, "I don't believe in that healing stuff." Does that make it any less effective to someone else's life who believes God's Word? You say, "But I haven't seen it, and I am still sick." That is because you are in a broken world, and we are in a war down here. We need to believe God's Word.

When you begin to encourage yourself in the Lord, you start to cause your environment to be saturated with truth. You think about the truth all the time, and you become fully convinced that you are going to live forever in Heaven. One day you are going to take that costume you call your body off and hang it up and then go on to glory. When you realize that death is not anything but a promotion, then you do not fear death anymore, and you learn to live.

If you are afraid, then it is limiting you, but what if the light of the Word of God was shining in your life to the point where you believed? What if you started to trust because you could see the realities of Jesus Christ in your life, and you could see and experience the fact that He is moving and working in your life? If this is the case, then you are going to become a spiritual giant because you cannot stay the same after that. Every time I encounter weakness, a surge of resurrection power comes into my life, and I have learned to live off of this cycle of finding out where I end and where God begins.

What is it that's bothering you and provoking you in your life? I do not know about you, but I get fed up with the devil, and it makes me want to torment *him*. To torment him, I have to know who my God is, and I have to know who I am, and I have to know where the devil belongs. You have to enforce every day who your God is, who you are, and where the devil's place is—and that is under your feet. The devil is going to wish that is all it was because he is going to the lake of fire, and he is going to long for the day when he was just under your feet. The devil is about to get his medicine and more, and he is about to get paid back for everything he did against you. When the light of the Gospel comes in, you begin to feel the liberty of the Spirit in a greater way.

The demons are full of darkness and are the biggest losers because they can never be redeemed, and all these entities know that they are never going to have another chance. They are all out to destroy God's creation and out to make life miserable for you because they are out and you are in. You are in the family of God, and you get access to everything that Jesus Christ bought back because you are a co-heir with Him (see Rom. 8:17). There is so much in Scripture that talks about our position in God through Christ Jesus. God has given us the authority to become sons of the living God (see John 1:12). That means we have been given authority in Jesus Christ, and we can use His name. Also, whatever we permit on the earth, it is permitted, and whatever we do not permit on earth, it is not allowed to stay.

And I will give you the keys of the kingdom of heaven, and whatever you bind on earth will be bound in heaven, and whatever you loose on earth will be loosed in heaven.

—MATTHEW 16:19

What do you think Jesus was saying when He said, *"Whatever you bind on earth will be bound, and whatever you loose will be loosed"*? Jesus was talking about the fact that He was buying you back, and you are going be part of the family, and that devils have to listen to you. The devils do not want you to know this.

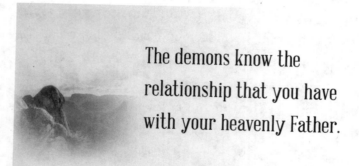

The demons know the relationship that you have with your heavenly Father.

You can make an impression in the spirit realm by your faith and trust in God. Demonic spirits will know that you fully understand your authority in Christ Jesus. The demons know the relationship that you have with your heavenly Father and how firmly convinced you are in what you believe. God is teaching you how to receive from Him and flow in the everlasting flow of God. When you let God's power flow out of you, the enemy does not want to be around you anymore.

Let the rivers of living water flow through you with the power of the Holy Spirit to transfer to others, to teach people, and to show them how to push back the enemy. When you yield to the Holy Spirit, you will receive the power from Heaven to transfer to earth. Nothing is impossible if you trust in God and learn to receive from His heavenly realms.

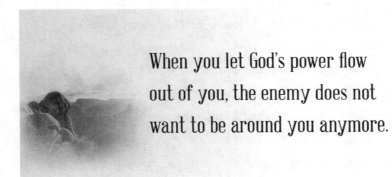

When you let God's power flow out of you, the enemy does not want to be around you anymore.

PRAYER OF IMPARTATION

The Lord says, "Your breakthrough is coming; it is scheduled. I have plans for you, plans for you to prosper. An expected end, a good end—I have plans for you. I sit in Heaven and laugh at your enemies because they are coming to nothing. My enemies are your enemies, and I have defeated them. I the Lord have come in your midst and I am mighty in your midst. Always worship Me, always recognize Me as being the Most High, for I am the High and Lofty One who inhabits eternity, but I also dwell with you, the humble and contrite in spirit, and I will walk with you. Those who fear Me I will withhold no good thing from them. I am your God. I will come and I will live with you. Your house will be different; your neighborhood will be different. Your work will be different. Everything will start to change as you allow the command from Heaven to come through you in authority. Trust Me this day. I am not going to withhold any good thing from you. I have come with a drawn sword. I am a Warrior," says the Lord. "I am singing songs of deliverance right now over you. I shall drive your enemies out; they will be no more. I the Lord have come. The powers of the coming age, healing to your body, healing to your mind, surges of glory in your spirit right now, receive from Heaven, receive the fire from the altar.

"I am your God; turn to Me. I am all you need; turn to Me and be set free—freedom, freedom, freedom. Where the Spirit of the Lord is, there is freedom. He whom the Son sets free is free indeed. Free to believe. Free to trust in your Father God. Free, you are free. You are healed. No one will touch you. The evil one will not touch you. You are in the shadow of the Most High, the secret place, and no evil shall touch you. The angels are

going out to your home. Everything about you will prosper. The angels will work on your behalf; they have been sent to serve you. For those who are going to inherit salvation, the angels will make sure that the favor of the Lord is predominant in your life. I am going to show Myself out through you. Everyone will know that I am with you," says the Lord. "You will prosper, and your lands shall prosper. Everything about you shall prosper."

Salvation Prayer

Lord God,

I confess that I am a sinner.

I confess that I need Your Son, Jesus.

Please forgive me in His name.

Lord Jesus, I believe You died for me and that You are alive and listening to me now.

I now turn from my sins and welcome You into my heart. Come and take control of my life.

Make me the kind of person You want me to be.

Now, fill me with Your Holy Spirit who will show me how to live for You. I acknowledge You before men as my Savior and my Lord.

In Jesus' name.

Amen.

If you prayed this prayer, please contact us at info@kevinzadai.com for more information and material. Go to KevinZadai.com for other exciting ministry materials.

Join our network at Warriornotes.tv. Join our ministry and training school at Warrior Notes School of Ministry.

Visit KevinZadai.com for more info.

ABOUT DR. KEVIN ZADAI

Kevin Zadai, Th.D. was called to ministry at the age of ten. He attended Central Bible College in Springfield, Missouri, where he received a bachelor of arts in theology. Later, he received training in missions at Rhema Bible College and a doctorate of theology from Primus University. He is currently ordained through Rev. Dr. Jesse and Rev. Dr. Cathy Duplantis. At age thirty-one, during a routine day surgery, he found himself on the "other side of the veil" with Jesus. For forty-five minutes, the Master revealed spiritual truths before returning him to his body and assigning him to a supernatural ministry. Kevin holds a commercial pilot license and is retired from Southwest Airlines after twenty-nine years as a flight attendant. Kevin is the founder and president of Warrior Notes School of Ministry. He and his lovely wife, Kathi, reside in New Orleans, Louisiana.